T0115205

STUDYING PROPHECY

Fulfillment Throughout History and Today

GLYNDA PATTON

WESTBOW
PRESS®
A DIVISION OF THOMAS NELSON
& ZONDERVAN

WestBow Press books may be ordered through booksellers or by contacting:

WestBow Press
A Division of Thomas Nelson & Zondervan
1663 Liberty Drive
Bloomington, IN 47403
www.westbowpress.com
844-714-3454

All Scripture quotations are taken from the King James Version.

ISBN: 978-1-6642-2975-4 (sc)
ISBN: 978-1-6642-2977-8 (hc)
ISBN: 978-1-6642-2976-1 (e)

Library of Congress Control Number: 2021906663

Print information available on the last page.

WestBow Press rev. date: 04/07/2021

To my supportive, loving husband, Brad, and my family and friends. Without you lifting me up with love and prayers, this book would not have been possible. May God bless and keep you always.

PREFACE

On many occasions I have been asked, "Why did you pick seminary to further your education?" or "Why do you focus your Bible studies on prophecy?" The answer begins like this …

At the age of twenty-two, I went to the altar and accepted Jesus as my own personal Savior. During this time, I was a young and immature child of God, battling the simple sowing of the seed (God's Holy Word). If you are asking what this means, let me explain.

Unlike most Christians at that time, I did not attend church from my youth. I had no Sunday school experience and no one had explained the Bible to me. Watching *The Ten Commandments* with Charlton Heston was the extent of my biblical education. By the way, the first time I read Exodus, I remember thinking, *Someone got this all wrong.*

When I first began my Christian journey, I could not get enough of God's Word and church. I attended service every Sunday morning and night, and every Wednesday evening service. I even taught children during summer vacation Bible school. However, because of my lack of understanding, Satan came and took the Word away by means of keeping my attention on other events happening in my life. Then the Word just fell away by lack of commitment. Soon the cares of the world choked out the Word, meaning that my own trials and tribulations became more important. This happened because of my own "sowing of the seed" experience, distracting me from continuing to nourish the Word and continuing my commitment to my studies and the worshipping of God (Matt. 13:3–9).

To get my attention, God gave me a powerful dream, which began my interest in the studies of the Second Coming of Jesus Christ. I found that in order to understand the end, one must start at the beginning. I noticed that the prophecies of Christ began in Genesis, the beginning of God's Word, and continues through Revelation.

By enrolling in seminary, I had the help I so desired to nourish the seed (God's Word). I felt I would grow deep roots and produce good fruit for my Father in heaven. Receiving my bachelor's degree in theology of biblical studies—the education I received—the message I now give to you, is not of my own doing. So that I might further the kingdom of God, the Holy Spirit gave me a profound desire to learn. To God be all the glory.

Today, I am still learning every day as I study and ask our Father for direction. I do believe that God has a special mission for me, and that mission is to tell people that His Son is coming, and soon. Sooner than we might think. I do not know when, not even Jesus knew the answer to that question when asked (Matt. 24:36). But He did give us some signs to look for before His Second Coming.

It is my prayer that with this study, people can see the signs and prepare their lamps filled with oil, because our Groom is coming for His bride.

TRADITION AND DOCTRINES

Within my preface, I wanted to make a special note. I came to the altar of God during a revival at a Free Will Baptist Church, where a Pentecostal preacher was preaching. It is my belief that this was not coincidental.

Over the years, I have studied under several different denominations with an open mind. Why? Because all too many times, we as Christians get caught up in traditional beliefs rather than truth. The scribes and Pharisees were caught up in their traditions and Jesus called them "vipers and snakes." They were so caught up in their traditions that they missed the Messiah. Let us learn from this and not make the same mistake.

INTRODUCTION

In the preface, I told you of a dream that directed my focus to the prophecies of Jesus's Second Coming. For many years I tried on my own to understand these prophecies. Finally, I decided to further my education in the seminary.

The more I eagerly read and studied God's Word, the more He chose to reveal to me. I completed notebook after notebook's worth of revelation.

I came to realize that a great deal of the prophecies of the Second Coming of Christ had been fulfilled in our history. By accumulating these fulfillments, I began to understand that a timeline was developing.

By the end of my studies, an urgency to share this knowledge intensified. It was this urgency that began as a study and ultimately developed into the book you are reading today.

I hope you enjoy this ride through history and prophecy fulfillment. It is my intent to reveal the scroll sealed by Daniel, which has been opening throughout our history, one seal at a time.

To aid in this study, I have included the scripture associated with each prophecy. All scripture in this book is from the King James Version because it was the first translation into the English language.

May God bless the reader with each chapter.

CHAPTER 1

STUDYING BIBLICAL PROPHECY

INTERPRETING THE BIBLE

Factual

- Fact 1: God indeed created the heavens and the earth and all things within. Genesis 1 gives us this history.
- Fact 2: There is a historical genealogy that can be traced from Adam to Jesus. Matthew 1:1–7 gives us the genealogy from Abraham to Jesus, and in Luke 3:23–38, we can see where Jesus's genealogy can be traced back to Adam.
- Fact 3: When the Dead Sea Scrolls were discovered, they gave proof to the laws of Moses and other scriptures within the Old Testament, which includes facts one and two, listed above.

The Dead Sea Scrolls were discovered between 1947 and 1956 in a series of eleven caves by the archaeological site of Qumran in the Judaean Desert, near the Dead Sea. The texts have great historical, religious, and linguistic significance because they include the second oldest known surviving manuscripts of written works, later included in the Hebrew Bible.

It is this Hebrew Bible, the Tanakh, that is our source of the laws of Moses that we study in the Old Testament of the Christian Bible. It is these Dead Sea Scrolls that help validate the Holy Bible. (Fulfillment of prophecies validates scripture.)

Almost all the Dead Sea Scrolls are held by the state of Israel in the Shrine of the Book on the grounds of the Israel Museum.

Prophetic

From Genesis to Revelation there are prophecies of Jesus, who is the center of all scripture. Genesis 3:15 is our first glimpse of prophecy, which is known as the protogospel. The first prophecy of Jesus Christ reads as follows: "And I will put enmity between thee and the woman, and between thy seed and her seed; it shall bruise thy head, and thou shall bruise his heel" (Gen. 3:15).

Symbolism

To understand the above prophecy, you first have to learn the symbolism associated with the verse. Today, the word *woman* refers to the church. However, in the Old Testament, it referred to the Israelites (God's chosen people): "I have likened the daughter of Zion to a lovely and delicate 'woman'" (Jer. 6:2).

The "seed of woman" references the genealogy of Adam to Jesus: "That is, those who are the children of the flesh, these are not the children of God; but the children of the promise are counted as the 'seed'" (Rom. 9:8).

The serpent is Satan, as seen in Revelation 20:2, which says, "'And he laid hold on the dragon, that old serpent, which is the Devil, and Satan, and bound him a thousand years.'"

The word *woman* is symbolic of the Israelites, God's chosen people. *Seed* is symbolic of genealogy. The serpent symbolizes Satan. By knowing the symbolism for these words, one can know the interpretation of the above verses. They mean that until Jesus comes, Satan will try to hinder or destroy the genealogy of Jesus, but Jesus *will* come and defeat Satan by defeating death, which Satan caused. Thereby, Jesus will take the keys of death from Satan and be resurrected to the right hand of God, from which Jesus *will* come again for us (John 14:2).

SECOND INTERPRETATION OF "SEED OF WOMAN"

Some theologians have an additional interpretation of Genius 3:15. They believe that the "seed of woman" is a virgin birth, because man is not mentioned. It is my opinion that this interpretation holds true value as well. It helps us understand how mythology begot paganism. This paganism is reveled within prophecy, so it is of importance.

Paganism began with Nimrod, to whom we are introduced in Genesis 10:8–12. Nimrod was a mighty warrior before the Lord. "And Cush begat Nimrod: he began to be a mighty one in the earth. He was a mighty hunter before the Lord: wherefore it is said, Even as Nimrod the mighty hunter before the Lord" (Gen. 10:8–9). In Hebrew, the phrase "a mighty one" is *gibbôr,* which means "powerful" and, by implication, "warrior" or "tyrant." It was Nimrod who began the Tower of Babel.

Nimrod builds the Tower of Babel because "he would be revenged on God if He should have a mind to drown the world again. For that he would build a tower too high for the waters to reach and that he would avenge himself on God for destroying their forefathers" (Josephus Book 1: chapter 4).

Josephus was a historian who wrote about the Jewish people. His works have contributed to our understanding of the social, political, and historical backgrounds of the New Testament era.

THE MYTH OF THE SUN GOD (FIRST PAGAN MYTH)

Nimrod marries a woman named Semiramis, who has an adulterous affair and conceives a child. At that time, Nimrod dies a horrible death. To hide the affair and remain in power, Semiramis declares that Nimrod had been resurrected as the god of the sun. As the sun god, he used his sun rays to miraculously inseminate Semiramis with a child. Thus, the son god was created—the first immaculate birth. This spread around the world, starting a birth, death, and rebirth cult of the sun god: the birth of paganism

The story of Nimrod and Semiramis is *not* in scripture. Nimrod and Semiramis's story is part of mythology. Mythology is important in prophecy because it is a tool that Satan used to confuse mankind, to cast doubt on the virgin birth and Jesus's immaculate conception. "Thou shall bruise His heel" (Gen. 3:15).

In prophecy, the chosen people of God, either the Israelites or Jesus's true church, mix mythology, or paganism, in with their teaching. Therefore, I have chosen to include this interpretation for educational purposes, as a tool for understanding "harlotry" in scripture.

IMPORTANCE OF STUDYING BIBLICAL PROPHECY

God Reveals

"Surely the Lord God will do nothing, but He revealeth His secret unto His servants the prophets" (Amos 3:7). What does this mean? Whenever God does anything significant in history, He always lets His people know in advance through either Himself or inspired men and women.

For example, before the world was destroyed by the flood, God Himself came as a messenger to warn Noah (Gen. 6:13; 7:1–10). Before the children of Israel went down into Egypt, God told Abraham that his descendants were going to go (Gen. 15:13). Before the Israelites came out of Egypt, God sent Moses (Ex. 3:2-10). Before Jerusalem was destroyed by the Babylonians, He sent Isaiah and Jeremiah (Is. 22:17; Jer. 6:8).

The first chapter in Revelation, reads, "The Revelation of Jesus Christ, which God gave unto Him, to shew unto His servants the things which must shortly come to pass; and He sent and signified it by His angel unto His servant John." This means that it came from God—the Father to Jesus—to the angel, to John, written for you and me today. God has given us advance notice.

God Blesses

We are told in Revelation 1:3 that we are blessed by reading this prophecy: "Blessed is he that readeth, and they that hear the words of this prophecy, and keep those things which are written therein; for the time is at hand."

God Cannot Lie

"God is not a man, that he should lie; neither the son of man, that he should repent: hath He spoken, and shall He not make it good" (Num. 23:9). When God speaks, things happen. Didn't God speak and creation began? "And God said, 'Let there be light,' and there was light."

It is impossible for God to lie. "That by two immutable things, in which it was impossible for God to lie" (Heb. 6:18).

God Is Omnipresent

You and I live in the present. God lives simultaneously in all parts of time. He is the alpha and the omega, the beginning and the end (Rev. 1:8). When He tells us something is going to happen, He's not guessing like the weatherman; He knows what's going to happen.

Matthew 24:35 says, "Heaven and earth shall pass away, but My Words shall not pass away." God's word is forever.

THE FULFILLMENT OF BIBLICAL PROPHECIES OF JESUS

There are more than three hundred Old Testament prophecies regarding the Messiah that were fulfilled when Jesus came. Here are a few examples:

The Birthplace

"But thou, Bethlehem Ephratah, though thou be little among the thousands of Judah, yet out of thee shall He come forth unto me that is to be ruler in Israel; whose goings forth have been from of old, from everlasting" (Mic. 5:2).

Born of a Virgin:

"Therefore, the Lord Himself shall give you a sign: Behold, a virgin shall conceive, and bear a son, and shall call his name Immanuel" (Isa. 7:14).

King Herod Trying to Murder Him

"Thus, saith the Lord, A voice was heard in Ramah, lamentation, and bitter weeping; Rachel weeping for her children refused to be comforted for her children, because they were not" (Jer. 31:15).

No Bones Broken

"He keepeth all His bones; not one of them is broken" (Ps. 34:20).

His Clothing Would Be Gambled For

"They part My garments among them and cast lots upon my vesture" (Ps. 22:18).

Buried in a Rich Man's Tomb

"And, He made His grave with the wicked, and with the rich in His death; because He had done no violence, neither was any deceit in His mouth". (Isaiah 53:9).

Raised on the Third Day

"After two days will He revive us: in the third day He will raise us up, and we shall live in His sight" (Hos. 6:2).

Just as predicted, Jesus came the first time. Remember that when Jesus came, God's people had been waiting 1,500 years for His coming. They had been waiting 2,000 years from the time of Abraham. They had begun to lose faith that the coming of their Messiah, Jesus, was ever going to transpire. Two thousand years after Jesus's first coming, the same thing is happening: some are losing faith that He will come.

CHAPTER 2

UNDERSTANDING PROPHECY

How to Understand Prophecy

As mentioned before, many of the Bible prophecies were written with symbols. Some of these prophecies were written during a time when God's people were captive in another country. The disciples of Christ were under the authority of Rome. Daniel was captive in Babylon, Ezekiel in Persia, and John on the isle of Patmos. Symbolic writings were intended to keep those writing them from being charged with treason while in occupied territory.

That means that in order to protect the message, the prophecies were written in symbolic language. The keys to unlock those symbols are within the Bible itself.

> He answered and said unto them, Because it is given unto you to know the mysteries of the kingdom of heaven, but to them it is not given; Therefore speak I to them in parables: because they seeing see not; and hearing they hear not, neither do they understand. (Matt. 13:11, 13)

The reader also must eagerly want to understand and ask our Heavenly Father for understanding. "Ask and it will be given to you, seek and you will find, knock and it will be opened unto you." (Matt. 7:7). Furthermore, the reader should be doing or eagerly wanting to do the will of the Father. "If any man will do His will, he shall know of the doctrine, whether it be of God, or whether I speak of myself" (John 7:17).

CENTRAL THEME IN PROPHECY

The central theme of prophecy is to point you and me to Jesus. It is redemptive in value. God wants us to know that He knows the future and that He has a plan for you and me. He is going to be the center of all the prophecies in this book.

"You search the Scriptures, for in them you think you have eternal life; and these are they which testify of Me" (John 5:39).

THE KEY TO UNDERSTANDING

The key to understanding prophecies in the Bible is to let the Bible interpret itself. You must compare scripture with scripture. This means you need to look in other places in the Bible to understand the symbolism in prophecy. It also means you need to know scriptures. Let us review some symbolic examples.

"He had in His right hand seven stars, out of His mouth went a sharp two-edged sword, and His countenance was like the sun shining in its strength" (Rev. 1:16). Does this mean when we get to heaven and see Jesus, He will have a saber sticking out of His mouth? No. Obviously this is symbolic.

"For *the word of God* is living and powerful, and sharper than any two-edged sword, piercing even to the division of soul and spirit, and of joints and marrow, and is a discerner of the thoughts and intents of the heart" (Heb. 4:12; emphasis mine). In this verse we can see the meaning of the sword: it is the word of God.

Several times in Revelation it talks about the Lamb that was slain. "*Behold the Lamb of God* that takes away the sin of the world" (John 1:29; emphasis mine). The symbolic meaning of the Lamb is Jesus.

In Revelation 17:3–6, we are introduced to a woman sitting on a beast that has seven heads and ten horns, coming up out of the sea. The woman is drunk with the blood of the saints. This does not mean an actual beastly animal is going to be coming out of the sea with a woman sitting on its back. It is symbolic. Let me explain.

Previously in symbolism, we learned that woman in the Old Testament meant God's chosen people (the Israelites) and the church in the New Testament. But this is a different kind of woman. One is pure, and one is corrupt. The corrupt woman is one who worships someone or something other than God. (Ez. 16:15–58, 23:2–21). The beast is a kingdom, government, or political power.

"Those great *beasts*, which are four, are four *kings* which arise out of the earth" (Dan. 7:17). "Thus, he said: *the fourth beast* shall be a fourth *kingdom* on earth, which shall be different from all the other kingdoms, and shall devour the whole earth, trample it and break it in pieces" (Dan. 7:23).

From this we can know that the woman here is a corrupt church and the beast is a kingdom, government, or political power. What does it mean to be drunk with the blood of the saints? It is persecution and martyrdom of the pure church.

Later we will go into this prophecy in more detail, as it has a great meaning in biblical prophecy.

In the rest of this chapter, you will find most of the commonly used words in scripture that have symbolic meanings. I also share where you can find that meaning in scripture.

ANIMALS

Horse—Strength and power in battle. "Hast thou given the horse strength? Hast thou clothed his neck with thunder?" (Job 39:19); "He delighteth not in the strength of the horse: he taketh not pleasure in the legs of a man" (Ps. 147:10); "The horse is prepared against the day of battle: but safety is of the Lord" (Prov.21:31).

Dragon—Satan or his agency. "In that day of the Lord with His sore and great and strong sword shall punish leviathan the piercing serpent, even leviathan that crooked serpent; and He shall slay the dragon that is in the sea" (Isa. 27:1); "The huge dragon, the ancient serpent, who is called the devil and Satan, who deceived the whole world, was thrown down to earth, and its angels were thrown down with it"; "And the great dragon was cast out, that old serpent, called the Devil, and Satan, which deceiveth the whole world: he was cast out into the earth, and his angels were cast out with him" (Rev. 12:7–9).

Beast—a kingdom, government, or political power. "These great beasts, which are four, and four kings, which shall arise out of the earth" (Dan. 7:17); "Thus he said, the fourth beast shall be the fourth kingdom upon earth, which shall be diverse from all kingdoms, and shall devour the whole earth, and shall tread it down, and break it in pieces" (Dan. 7:23).

Lamb—Jesus, sacrifice. "The next day John seeth Jesus coming unto him, and saith, Behold the Lamb of God, which taketh away the sin of the world" (John 1:29); "Purge out therefore the old leaven, that ye may be a new lump, as ye are unleavened. For even Christ our Passover is sacrificed for us" (1 Cor. 5:7).

Lion—Jesus or powerful king (e.g., Babylon). "And I wept much, because no man was found worthy to open and to read the book, neither to look thereon. And one of the elders saith unto me, weep not: behold, the Lion of the tribe of Judah, the Root of David, hath prevailed to open the book, and to lose the seven seals thereof. And I beheld, and, lo, in the midst of the throne and of the four beasts, and I the midst of the elders, stood a Lamb as it had been slain," (Rev.5:4–9); "The first was like a lion, and had eagle's wings" (Dan. 7:4); "These great beasts, which are four, are four kings, which shall arise out of the earth" (Dan 7:17); "Thus he said, the fourth beast shall be the fourth kingdom upon earth, which shall be diverse from all kingdom's, and shall devour the whole earth, and shall tread it down, and break it in pieces" (Dan. 7:23). See also Jeremiah 50:43–44.

Bear—Destructive power or Medo-Persia. "[A]s a roaring lion, and a ranging bear; so is a wicked ruler over the poor people" (Prov. 28:15); "And he went up from thence unto Bethel: and as he was going up by the way, there came forth little children out of the city, and mocked him, and said unto him; go up, thou bald head. And he turned back, and looked on them, and cursed them in the name of the LORD. And there came forth two she bears out of the wood, and tare forty and two children of them" (2 Kings 2:23–24); "And behold another beast, a second, like to a bear, and it raised up itself on one side, and it had three ribs in the mouth of it between the teeth of it: and they said thus unto it, Arise, devour much flesh" (Dan. 7:5).

Leopard—Greece. "After this I beheld, and lo another, like a leopard, which had upon the back of it four wings of a fowl; the beast had also four heads; and dominion was given to it" (Dan. 7:6).

Serpent—Satan. "And the great dragon was cast out, that old serpent, called the Devil, and Satan, which deceiveth the whole world: he was cast out into the earth, and his angels were cast out with him" (Rev. 12:9); "And he laid hold on the dragon, that old serpent, which is the Devil, and Satan, and bound him a thousand years" (Rev. 20:2).

Wolf—Disguised enemy that hunts in a time of darkness. *"Beware of false prophets, which come to you in sheep's clothing, but inwardly they are ravening wolves"* (Matt. 7:15).

Dove—Holy Spirit. "And straightway coming up out of the water, he saw the heavens opened, and the Spirit like a dove descending upon him" (Mark 1:10).

Ram—Medo-Persia: "The ram which thou sawest having two horns are the kings of Media and Persia" (Dan. 8:20).

Goat—Greece. "And the rough goat is the king of Grecia: and the great horn that is between his eyes is the first king" (Dan. 8:21).

Parts of Animals

Horn—King or kingdom. "And the ten horns out of this kingdom are ten kings that shall arise: and another shall rise after them; and he shall be diverse from the first, and he shall subdue three kings" (Dan. 7:24); "And as I was considering, behold, and the goat came from the west on the face of the whole earth, and touched not the ground: and the goat had a notable horn between his eyes" (Dan. 8:5); "And the rough goat is the king of Grecia: and the great horn that is between his eyes is the first king. Now that being broken, whereas four" (Dan. 8:21–22). See also Zechariah 1:18–19 and Revelation 17:12).

Wings—Speed or protection or deliverance. "The LORD shall bring a nation against thee from far, from the end of the earth, as swift as the eagle flieth; a nation whose tongue thou shalt not understand" (Deut. 28:49); "O Jerusalem, Jerusalem, thou that killest the prophets, and stonest them which are sent unto thee, how often would I have gathered thy children together, even as a hen gathereth her chickens under her wings, and ye would not!" (Matt. 23:37).

Objects

Gold—Pure character or precious and rare. "I will make a man more precious than fine gold; even a man than the golden wedge of Ophir" (Isa. 13:12).

Silver—Pure words and understanding. "If thou seekest her as silver, and searchest for her as for hid treasures" (Prov. 2:4); "Happy is the man that findeth wisdom, and the man that getteth understanding. For the merchandise of it is better than the merchandise of silver, and the gain thereof than fine gold" (Prov. 3:13–14). See also Proverbs 10:20, 25:11 and Psalms 12:6.

Brass, Tin, Iron, or Lead—Impure character. "As they gather silver, and brass, and iron, and lead, and tin, into the midst of the furnace, to blow the fire upon it, to melt it; so will I gather you in mine anger and in my fury, and I will leave you there, and melt you. Yea, I will gather you, and blow upon you in the fire of my wrath, and ye shall be melted in the midst thereof" (Ez. 22:20–21).

Water—Holy Spirit or everlasting life. "He that believeth on me, as the scripture hath said, out of his belly shall flow rivers of living water. (But this spake he of the Spirit, which they that believe on him should receive: for the Holy Ghost was not yet given; because that Jesus was not yet glorified)" (John 7:38–39); "But whosoever drinketh of the water that I shall give him shall never thirst; but the water that I shall give him shall be in him a well of water springing up into everlasting life" (John 4:14). See also Revelation 22:17 and Ephesians 5:26.

Waters—Inhabited area or people and nations. "And he saith unto me, The waters which thou sawest, where the whore sitteth, are peoples, and multitudes, and nations, and tongues" (Rev. 17:15).

Fire—Holy Spirit. "John answered, saying unto them all, I indeed baptize you with water; but one mightier than I cometh, the latchet of whose shoes I am not worthy to unloose: he shall baptize you with the Holy Ghost and with fire" (Luke 3:16).

Tree—Cross or people and nation. "The righteous shall flourish like the palm tree: he shall grow like a cedar in Lebanon" (Ps.92:12); "I have seen the wicked in great power and spreading himself like a green bay tree" (Ps. 37:35).

Seed—Descendants or Jesus. "That is, They which are the children of the flesh, these are not the children of God: but the children of the promise are counted for the seed" (Rom. 9:8); "Now to Abraham and his seed were the promises made. He saith not, and to seeds, as of many; but as of one, and to thy seed, which is Christ" (Gal. 3:16).

Fruit—Works or actions. "But the fruit of the Spirit is love, joy, peace, longsuffering, gentleness, goodness, faith" (Gal. 5:22).

Fig Tree—A nation that should bear fruit. "He spake also this parable; A certain man had a fig tree planted in his vineyard; and he came and sought fruit thereon and found none. Then said he unto the dresser of his vineyard, Behold, these three years I come seeking fruit on this fig tree, and find none: cut it down; why cumbereth it the ground? And he answering said unto him, Lord, let it alone this year also, till I shall dig about it, and dung it: And if it bear fruit, well: and if not, then after that thou shalt cut it down" (Luke 13:6–9).

Vineyard—Church that should bear fruit. "Then began He to speak to the people this parable; 'A certain man planted a vineyard, and let it forth to husbandmen, and went into a far country for a long time. And at the season he sent a servant to the husbandmen, that they should give him of the fruit of the vineyard: but the husbandmen beat him and sent him away empty. And, again he sent another servant: and they beat him also, and entreated him shamefully, and sent him away empty. And again, he sent a third: and they wounded him also and cast him out'" (Luke 20:9–12).

Field—The world. "The field is the world; the good seed are the children of the kingdom; but the tares are the children of the wicked one" (Matt. 13:38); "Say not ye, There are yet four months, and then cometh harvest? behold, I say unto you, Lift up your eyes, and look on the fields; for they are white already to harvest" (John 4:35).

Harvest—The end of the world. "The enemy that sowed them is the devil; the harvest is the end of the world; and the reapers are the angels" (Matt. 13:39).

Reapers—Angels. "The enemy that sowed them is the devil; the harvest is the end of the world; and the reapers are the angels" (Matt. 13:39).

Thorns, Thorny Ground—Cares of this life. "And these are they which are sown among thorns; such as hear the word, And the cares of this world, and the deceitfulness of riches, and the lusts of other things entering in, choke the word, and it becometh unfruitful" (Mark 4:18–19).

Stars—Angels or messengers. "And he had in his right hand seven stars: and out of his mouth went a sharp two-edged sword: and his countenance was as the sun shineth in his strength. The mystery of the seven stars which thou sawest in my right hand, and the seven golden candlesticks. The seven stars are the angels of the seven churches: and the seven candlesticks which thou sawest are the seven churches" (Rev.1:16, 20); "And his tail drew the third part of the stars of heaven, and did cast them to the earth: and the dragon stood before the woman which was ready to be delivered, for to devour her child as soon as it was born." And there was war in heaven: Michael and his angels fought against the dragon; and the dragon fought and his angels, And prevailed not; neither was their place found any more in heaven. And the great dragon was cast out, that old serpent, called the Devil, and Satan, which deceiveth the whole world: he was cast out into the earth, and his angels were cast out with him" (Rev. 12:4, 7–9); See also Job 38:7.

Jordan—Death. "But I must die in this land, I must not go over Jordan: but ye shall go over and possess that good land" (Deut. 4:22); "Therefore we are buried with him by baptism into death: that like as Christ was raised up from the dead by the glory of the Father, even so we also should walk in newness of life" (Rom. 6:4). To enter the promised land, the Israelites had to cross the Jordan River, symbolic of death to sin, just as they went through the Red Sea, symbolic of baptism, death, and new live.

Mountains—Political or religious political powers. "And it shall come to pass in the last days, that the mountain_of_the_LORD'S_house shall be established in the top of the mountains and shall be exalted above the hills; and all nations shall flow unto it. And many people shall go and say, Come ye, and let us go up to the mountain of the LORD, to the house of the God of Jacob; and he will teach us of his ways, and we will walk in his paths: for out of Zion shall go forth the law, and the word of the LORD from Jerusalem" (Isa. 2:2–3); "O my mountain in the field, I will give thy substance and all thy treasures to the spoil, and thy high places for sin, throughout all thy borders" (Jer. 17:3); "Then was the iron, the clay, the brass, the silver, and the gold, broken to pieces together, and became like the chaff of the summer threshing floors; and the wind carried them away, that no place was found for them: and the stone that smote the image became a great mountain, and filled the whole earth" (Dan. 2:35); "And in the days of these kings shall the God of heaven set up a kingdom, which shall never be destroyed: and the kingdom shall not be left to other people, but it shall break in pieces and consume all these kingdoms, and it shall stand for ever. Forasmuch as thou sawest that the stone was cut out of the mountain without hands, and that it brake in pieces the iron, the brass, the clay, the silver, and the gold; the great God hath made known to the king what shall come to pass hereafter: and the dream is certain, and the interpretation thereof sure" (Dan. 2:44–45). See also Jeremiah 31:23, 51:24–25 and Ezekiel 17:22–23).

Rock—Jesus or truth. "And did all drink the same spiritual drink: for they drank of that spiritual Rock that followed them: and that Rock was Christ" (1 Cor. 10:4); "As it is written, Behold, I lay in Sion a stumbling stone and rock of offence: and whosoever believeth on him shall not be ashamed" (Rom. 9:33); "Therefore whosoever heareth these sayings of mine, and doeth them, I will liken him unto a wise man, which built his house upon a rock" (Matt. 7:24).

Sun—Jesus or the Gospel. "For the LORD God is a sun and shield: the LORD will give grace and glory: no good thing will he withhold from them that walk uprightly" (Ps. 84;11); "But unto you that fear my name shall the Sun of righteousness arise with healing in his wings; and ye shall go forth and grow up as calves of the stall" (Mal. 4:2); "And was transfigured before them: and His face did shine as the sun, and his raiment was white as the light" (Matt. 17:2). See also John 8:12; 9:5.

Winds—Strife, commotion, or winds of war. "A noise shall come even to the ends of the earth; for the LORD hath a controversy with the nations, he will plead with all flesh; he will give them that are wicked to the sword, saith the LORD. Thus, saith the LORD of hosts, Behold, evil shall go forth from nation to nation, and a great whirlwind shall be raised up from the coasts of the earth. And the slain of the LORD shall be at that day from one end of the earth even unto the other end of the earth: they shall not be lamented, neither gathered, nor buried; they shall be dung upon the ground" (Jer. 25:31–33); "And upon Elam will I bring the four winds from the four quarters of heaven and will scatter them toward all those winds; and there shall be no nation whither the outcasts of Elam shall not come. For I will cause Elam to be dismayed before their enemies, and before them that seek their life: and I will bring evil upon them, even my fierce anger, saith the LORD; and I will send the sword after them, till I have consumed them" (Jer. 49:36–37). See also Jeremiah 4:11–13 and Zechariah 7:14.

COLORS

White—Purity. "And the great dragon was cast out, that old serpent, called the Devil, and Satan, which deceiveth the whole world: he was cast out into the earth, and his angels were cast out with him" (Rev. 12:9); "And white robes were given unto every one of them; and it was said unto them, that they should rest yet for a little season, until their fellow servants also and their brethren, that should be killed as they were, should be fulfilled" (Rev. 6:7).

Blue—Law. "Speak unto the children of Israel, and bid them that they make them fringes in the borders of their garments throughout their generations, and that they put upon the fringe of the borders a ribband of blue: And it shall be unto you for a fringe, that ye may look upon it, and remember all the commandments of the LORD, and do them; and that ye seek not after your own heart and your own eyes, after which ye use to go a whoring" (Num. 15:38–39).

Purple—Royalty. "And they clothed him with purple, and platted a crown of thorns, and put it about his head" (Mark 15:17); "And the weight of the golden earrings that he requested was a thousand and seven hundred shekels of gold; beside ornaments, and collars, and purple raiment that was on the kings of Midian, and beside the chains that were about their camels' necks" (Judg. 8:26).

Red/Scarlet—Sin or corruption. "Come now, and let us reason together, saith the LORD: though your sins be as scarlet, they shall be as white as snow; though they be red like crimson, they shall be as wool" (Isa. 1:18); "The shield of his mighty men is made red, the valiant men are in scarlet: the chariots shall be with flaming torches in the day of his preparation, and the fir trees shall be terribly shaken" (Nah. 2:3); "And there came one of the seven angels which had the seven vials, and talked with me, saying unto me, come hither; I will shew unto thee the judgment of the great whore that sitteth upon many waters: With whom the kings of the earth have committed fornication, and the inhabitants of the earth have been made drunk with the wine of her fornication. So, he carried me away in the spirit into the wilderness: and I saw a woman sit upon a scarlet coloured beast, full of names of blasphemy, having seven heads and ten horns" (Rev. 17:1–4).

PEOPLE AND BODY PARTS

Woman, Purity—God's chosen people or the true church. "I have likened the daughter of Zion to a comely and delicate woman" (Jer. 6:2); "For I am jealous over you with godly jealousy: for I have espoused you to one husband, that I may present you as a chaste virgin to Christ" (2 Cor. 11:2). See also Ephesians 5:23–27.

Woman, Corruption—Apostate church. "For their mother hath played the harlot: she that conceived them hath done shamefully: for she said, I will go after my lovers, that give me my bread and my water, my wool and my flax, mine oil and my drink" (Hos. 2:5); "Then said the LORD unto me, Go yet, love a woman beloved of her friend, yet an adulteress, according to the love of the LORD toward the children of Israel, who look to other gods, and love flagons of wine" (Hos. 3:1). See also Ezekiel 16:15–58, 23:2–21.

Thief—Suddenness of Jesus's coming. "For yourselves know perfectly that the day of the Lord so cometh as a thief in the night. For when they shall say, Peace and safety; then sudden destruction cometh upon them, as travail upon a woman with child; and they shall not escape. But ye, brethren, are not in darkness, that that day should overtake you as a thief" (1 Thess. 5:2–4); "But the day of the Lord will come as a thief in the night; in the which the heavens shall pass away with a great noise, and the elements shall melt with fervent heat, the earth also and the works that are therein shall be burned up" (2 Pet. 3:10).

Hand—Deeds, works, or actions. "Whatsoever thy hand findeth to do, do it with thy might; for there is no work, nor device, nor knowledge, nor wisdom, in the grave, whither thou goest" (Eccles. 9:10); "Their webs shall not become garments, neither shall they cover themselves with their works: their works are works of iniquity, and the act of violence is in their hands" (Isa. 59:6).

Forehead—Mind. "And these words, which I command thee this day, shall be in thine heart: And thou shalt teach them diligently unto thy children, and shalt talk of them when thou sittest in thine house, and when thou walkest by the way, and when thou liest down, and when thou risest up. And thou shalt bind them for a sign upon thine hand, and they shall be as frontlets between thine eyes" (Deut. 6:6–8); "I thank God through Jesus Christ our Lord. So then with the mind I myself serve the law of God; but with the flesh the law of sin" (Rom. 7:25). See also Ezekiel 3:8–9.

Feet—Your walk or direction. "And he said, behold now, my lords, turn in, I pray you, into your servant's house, and tarry all night, and wash your feet, and ye shall rise up early, and go on your ways. And they said, Nay; but we will abide in the street all night" (Gen. 19:2); "Thy word is a lamp unto my feet, and a light unto my path" (Ps. 119:105).

Eyes—Spiritual discernment. "But he that hateth his brother is in darkness, and walketh in darkness, and knoweth not whither he goeth, because that darkness hath blinded his eyes" (1 John 2:11). See also Matthew 13:10–17.

Skin—Christ's righteousness. "But with the precious blood of Christ, as of a lamb without blemish and without spot" (1 Pet. 1:19); "Your lamb shall be without blemish, a male of the first year: ye shall take it out from the sheep, or from the goats" (Exod. 12:5). See also Isaiah 1:4–6.

Tongue—Language or speech. "And Moses said unto the LORD, O my Lord, I am not eloquent, neither heretofore, nor since thou hast spoken unto thy servant: but I am slow of speech, and of a slow tongue" (Exod. 4:10).

Harlot—Apostate church or religion. "How is the faithful city become an harlot! it was full of judgment; righteousness lodged in it; but now murderers. Thy silver is become dross, thy wine mixed with water: Thy princes are rebellious, and companions of thieves: everyone loveth gifts, and followeth after rewards: they judge not the fatherless, neither doth the cause of the widow come unto them. Therefore saith the Lord, the LORD of hosts, the mighty One of Israel, Ah, I will ease me of mine adversaries, and avenge me of mine enemies: And I will turn my hand upon thee, and purely purge away thy dross, and take away all thy tin: And I will restore thy judges as at the first, and thy counsellors as at the beginning: afterward thou shalt be called, The city of righteousness, the faithful city. Zion shall be redeemed with judgment, and her converts with righteousness" (Isa. 1:21–27). See also Jeremiah 3:1–3, 6–9.

Heads—Major powers, rulers, or governments. "So he carried me away in the spirit into the wilderness: and I saw a woman sit upon a scarlet coloured beast, full of names of blasphemy, having seven heads and ten horns" (Rev. 17:3); "And here is the mind which hath wisdom. The seven heads are seven mountains, on which the woman sitteth. And there are seven kings: five are fallen, and one is, and the other is not yet come; and when he cometh, he must continue a short space" (Rev. 17:9–10).

ACTIONS AND AFFLICTIONS

Healing—Salvation. "Whether is easier, to say, thy sins be forgiven thee; or to say, Rise up and walk? But that ye may know that the Son of man hath power upon earth to forgive sins, (he said unto the sick of the palsy,) I say unto thee, Arise, and take up thy couch, and go into thine house" (Luke 5:23–24).

Leprosy/Sickness—Sin. "Whether is easier, to say, Thy sins be forgiven thee; or to say, Rise up and walk? But that ye may know that the Son of man hath power upon earth to forgive sins, (he said unto the sick of the palsy,) I say unto thee, Arise, and take up thy couch, and go into thine house" (Luke 5:23–24).

Famine—Death of truth. "Behold, the days come, saith the Lord GOD, that I will send a famine in the land, not a famine of bread, nor a thirst for water, but of hearing the words of the LORD" (Amos 8:11).

MISCELLANEOUS OBJECTS

Lamp—The Word of God. "Thy word is a lamp unto my feet, and a light unto my path" (Ps. 119:105).

Oil—The Holy Spirit. "And out of the throne proceeded lightnings and thunderings and voices: and there were seven lamps of fire burning before the throne, which are the seven Spirits of God" (Rev. 4:5). See also Zechariah 4:2–6.

Sword—Word of God. "And take the helmet of salvation, and the sword of the Spirit, which is the word of God" (Eph. 6:17); "For the word of God is quick, and powerful, and sharper than any two-edged sword, piercing even to the dividing asunder of soul and spirit, and of the joints and marrow, and is a discerner of the thoughts and intents of the heart" (Heb. 4:12).

Bread— Word of God. "And Jesus said unto them, I am the bread of life: he that cometh to me shall never hunger; and he that believeth on me shall never thirst" (John 6:35); "I am the living bread which came down from heaven: if any man eat of this bread, he shall live for ever: and the bread that I will give is my flesh, which I will give for the life of the world" (John 6:51).

Wine—Blood, covenant, or doctrines. "And no man putteth new wine into old bottles; else the new wine will burst the bottles, and be spilled, and the bottles shall perish" (Luke 5:37).

Honey—Happy life. "In the day that I lifted up mine hand unto them, to bring them forth of the land of Egypt into a land that I had espied for them, flowing with milk and honey, which is the glory of all lands" (Ez. 20:6); "A land of wheat, and barley, and vines, and fig trees, and pomegranates; a land of oil olive, and honey; A land wherein thou shalt eat bread without scarceness, thou shalt not lack any thing in it; a land whose stones are iron, and out of whose hills thou mayest dig brass" (Deut. 8:8–9).

Clothing—Character. "But we are all as an unclean thing, and all our righteousnesses are as filthy rags; and we all do fade as a leaf; and our iniquities, like the wind, have taken us away" (Isa. 64:6); "Their webs shall not become garments, neither shall they cover themselves with their works: their works are works of iniquity, and the act of violence is in their hands" (Isa. 59:6).

Crown—A glorious ruler or rulership. "The hoary head is a crown of glory, if it be found in the way of righteousness" (Prov. 16:31); "In that day shall the LORD of hosts be for a crown of glory, and for a diadem of beauty, unto the residue of his people" (Isa. 28:5); "Thou shalt also be a crown of glory in the hand of the LORD, and a royal diadem in the hand of thy God" (Isa. 62:3).

Ring—Authority. "And Pharaoh took off his ring from his hand, and put it upon Joseph's hand, and arrayed him in vestures of fine linen, and put a gold chain about his neck; And he made him to ride in the second chariot which he had; and they cried before him, Bow the knee: and he made him ruler over all the land of Egypt" (Gen. 41:42–43); "And the king took his ring from his hand, and gave it unto Haman the son of Hammedatha the Agagite, the Jews' enemy. And the king said unto Haman, the silver is given to thee, the people also, to do with them as it seemeth good to thee" (Est. 3:10–11).

Angel—Messenger. "And I heard a man's voice between the banks of Ulai, which called, and said, Gabriel, make this man to understand the vision" (Dan. 8:16); "Yea, whiles I was speaking in prayer, even the man Gabriel, whom I had seen in the vision at the beginning, being caused to fly swiftly, touched me about the time of the evening oblation" (Dan. 9:21); "And the angel answering said unto him, I am Gabriel, that stand in the presence of God; and am sent to speak unto thee, and to shew thee these glad tidings" (Luke 1:19, 26). See also Hebrews 1:14.

Babylon—Apostasy, confusion, or rebellion. "And he cried mightily with a strong voice, saying, Babylon the great is fallen, is fallen, and is become the habitation of devils, and the hold of every foul spirit, and a cage of every unclean and hateful bird. For all nations have drunk of the wine of the wrath of her fornication, and the kings of the earth have committed fornication with her, and the merchants of the earth are waxed rich through the abundance of her delicacies" (Rev. 18:2–3); "And there came one of the seven angels which had the seven vials, and talked with me, saying unto me, Come hither; I will shew unto thee the judgment of the great whore that sitteth upon many waters: With whom the kings of the earth have committed fornication, and the inhabitants of the earth have been made drunk with the wine of her fornication. So he carried me away in the spirit into the wilderness: and I saw a woman sit upon a scarlet coloured beast, full of names of blasphemy, having seven heads and ten horns. And the woman was arrayed in purple and scarlet colour, and decked with gold and precious stones and pearls, having a golden cup in her hand full of abominations and filthiness of her fornication: And upon her forehead was a name written, MYSTERY, BABYLON THE GREAT, THE MOTHER OF HARLOTS AND ABOMINATIONS OF THE EARTH" (Rev. 17:1–5).

Mark—Sign or seal of approval or disapproval. "And the LORD said unto him, Go through the midst of the city, through the midst of Jerusalem, and set a mark upon the foreheads of the men that sigh and that cry for all the abominations that be done in the midst thereof" (Ez. 9:4); "And he received the sign of circumcision, a seal of the righteousness of the faith which he had yet being uncircumcised: that he might be the father of all them that believe, though they be not circumcised; that righteousness might be imputed unto them also" (Rom. 4:11). See also Revelation 13:17, 14:9–11, 7:2–3.

Seal—Sign or mark of approval or disapproval. "And he received the sign of circumcision, a seal of the righteousness of the faith which he had yet being uncircumcised: that he might be the father of all them that believe, though they be not circumcised; that righteousness might be imputed unto them also" (Rom 4:11); "And I saw another angel ascending from the east, having the seal of the living God: and he cried with a loud voice to the four angels, to whom it was given to hurt the earth and the sea, Saying, Hurt not the earth, neither the sea, nor the trees, till we have sealed the servants of our God in their foreheads" (Rev. 7:2–3).

White Robes—Victory or righteousness. "And to her was granted that she should be arrayed in fine linen, clean and white: for the fine linen is the righteousness of saints" (Rev. 19:8); "He that overcometh, the same shall be clothed in white raiment; and I will not blot out his name out of the book of life, but I will confess his name before my Father, and before his angels" (Rev. 3:5); "And I said unto him, Sir, thou knowest. And he said to me, These are they which came out of great tribulation, and have washed their robes, and made them white in the blood of the Lamb" (Rev. 7:14).

Jar or Vessel—Person. "The word which came to Jeremiah from the LORD, saying, Arise, and go down to the potter's house, and there I will cause thee to hear my words. Then I went down to the potter's house, and, behold, he wrought a work on the wheels. And the vessel that he made of clay was marred in the hand of the potter: so he made it again another vessel, as seemed good to the potter to make it" (Jer.18:1–4); "But we have this treasure in earthen vessels, that the excellency of the power may be of God, and not of us" (2 Cor. 4:7).

Time—360 days. "And he shall speak great words against the most High, and shall wear out the saints of the most High, and think to change times and laws: and they shall be given into his hand until a time and times and the dividing of time" (Dan. 7:25); "And your children shall wander in the wilderness forty years, and bear your whoredoms, until your carcasses be wasted in the wilderness. After the number of the days in which ye searched the land, even forty days, each day for a year, shall ye bear your iniquities, even forty years, and ye shall know my breach of promise" (Num. 14:33–34).

Times—720 days. "And he shall speak great words against the most High, and shall wear out the saints of the most High, and think to change times and laws: and they shall be given into his hand until a time and times and the dividing of time" (Dan. 7:25); "And the woman fled into the wilderness, where she hath a place prepared of God, that they should feed her there a thousand two hundred and threescore days. And to the woman were given two wings of a great eagle, that she might fly into the wilderness, into her place, where she is nourished for a time, and times, and half a time, from the face of the serpent" (Rev. 12:6, 14); "And there was given unto him a mouth speaking great things and blasphemies; and power was given unto him to continue forty and two months" (Rev. 13:5).

Day—Literal year. "And when thou hast accomplished them, lie again on thy right side, and thou shalt bear the iniquity of the house of Judah forty days: I have appointed thee each day for a year" (Ez. 4:6); "After the number of the days in which ye searched the land, even forty days, each day for a year, shall ye bear your iniquities, even forty years, and ye shall know my breach of promise" (Num. 14:34).

Trumpet—Loud warning of God's approach. "And it came to pass on the third day in the morning, that there were thunders and lightnings, and a thick cloud upon the mount, and the voice of the trumpet exceeding loud; so that all the people that was in the camp trembled. And Moses brought forth the people out of the camp to meet with God; and they stood at the nether part of the mount" (Exod. 19:16–17); "And seven priests shall bear before the ark seven trumpets of rams' horns: and the seventh day ye shall compass the city seven times, and the priests shall blow with the trumpets. And it shall come to pass, that when they make a long blast with the ram's horn, and when ye hear the sound of the trumpet, all the people shall shout with a great shout; and the wall of the city shall fall down flat, and the people shall ascend up every man straight before him" (Josh. 6:4–5).

ASSURANCE OF JESUS SECOND COMING

"In My Father's house are many mansions; if it were not so, I would have told you. I go to prepare a place for you. And if I go and prepare a place for you, I will come again and receive you to Myself; that where I am, there you may be also" (John 14:2–3).

If Jesus told us He was coming back for us, we can be assured of this, as He cannot lie, because He and the Father are the same. "I and My Father are one" (John 10:30). As mentioned in chapter one, God cannot lie.

CONFIRMATION

> And after He said these things, He was lifted up while they were looking on, and a cloud received Him out of their sight. And as they were gazing intently into the sky while He was going, behold, two men in white clothing stood beside them. They also said, "Men of Galilee, why do you stand looking into the sky? This Jesus, who you have been taken up from you into heaven, will come in just the same way as you have watched Him go into heaven." (Acts 1:9–11)

CHAPTER 3

PROPHECY REVEALED WITHIN HISTORY AND MATH

History

Bible prophecy in history includes creation, the fall of man, and the genealogy of Jesus and the early church. Written within this genealogy are prophecies of what we are to look for in the coming Messiah, Jesus Christ. Both His first coming, which has been fulfilled in the fullness of time (Gal. 4:4–5), and the Second Coming, which will come in the fullness of time.

With our known history, we can also see fulfillment of some of the foretold prophecies of His Second Coming. Through seeing the foretold prophecies fulfilled, we receive confirmation of the truth of these prophecies. Later we will match our known history with prophecy, checking off the prophecies that have been fulfilled.

History of the Laws of Moses

On Mount Sinai, when God wrote the Ten Commandments with His own finger, He gave Moses what are called the laws of Moses. These laws are written in the books of Genesis, Exodus, Leviticus, Numbers, and Deuteronomy. The Ten Commandments are God's commandments to mankind. The laws of Moses are rules God gave to

Moses to be observed by the Israelites (God's chosen people). Those who have been washed by the blood of the Lamb, Jesus, have been adopted into the Israelite family (Gal. 3:29, 4:6–7).

HISTORY OF CREATION

In Genesis chapter 1, Moses tells us that God is our Creator. Chapter 1 also gives us a history of what God created, when He created it, and what His creation was for (Gen. 1:27–31).

HISTORY OF THE FALL OF MAN

Genesis chapter 3 gives us an account of why Jesus, the Son of God and the center of scripture, had to come to earth and die for our sins. This chapter is called "the fall of man" (Rom. 5:17).

THE BEGINNING OF JESUS'S GENEALOGY

Genesis chapter 5 gives us the beginning of Jesus's genealogy, "the seed of woman," a record of Adam and his descendants to Noah.

GENEALOGY CONTINUES

Genesis chapter 11 gives us the genealogy from Shem, son of Noah, to Abram, later Abraham (father of many nations), whom God blessed in Genesis chapter 15. The remaining chapters of Genesis give us a history of Abraham's descendants and the twelve sons of Jacob (Israel) who make up the twelve tribes of the Israelites.

This genealogy continues throughout the Old Testament and is repeated for us in Matthew chapter 1 and Luke chapter 3. To list them all would take another book entirely.

MATH

How better to tell the fullness of time but by math? Genesis begins with numbers and math, as it took six days for creation and a day of rest, making a total of seven (completion). With math, we can calculate the year of Adam's birth, the year of the flood, and the year of the exodus.

WHY IS TIME IMPORTANT?

Everything in scripture is there to educate us and give us hope. "For whatever was written in earlier times was written for our instruction, so that through perseverance and the encouragement of the Scriptures we might have hope" (Rom. 15:4). Jesus came in fullness of *time* (Gal. 4:4–5) and will return the same. Therefore, time is an important part of scripture and prophecy.

Furthermore, we were told that on the fourth day of creation God created the sun, moon, and stars to tell us <u>time</u>. "Let them be for signs and seasons, and for days and years" (Gen. 1:14). Math is required to determine time. This leads me to believe time is important to God.

SOLOMON'S REIGN TO THE EXODUS

"Now it came about in the four hundred and eightieth year, after the sons of Israel came out of Egypt, in the fourth year of Solomon's reign over Israel, in the month of Ziv which is the second month, that he (Solomon) began to build the house of the Lord" (1 Kings 6:1). It is well established that Solomon began his reign in 970 BC So by subtracting the four years (it was the fourth year of his reign), we can find the year that he started building the temple: 966 BC Now add 480 (the verse says it was 480 years after the Israelites left Egypt), and you get 1446 BC as the year of the exodus.

THE EXODUS TO ADAM'S BIRTH

The Israelites were in Egypt for 430 years: "Now the time that the sons of Israel lived in Egypt was four hundred and thirty years" (Exod. 12:40). Adding 1446 to 430 gives us 1876. So 1876 BC was the year the Israelites entered Egypt. When Jacob (Israel) entered Egypt, he tells the Pharaoh he is 130 years old: "So Jacob said to Pharaoh, 'The years of my sojourning are one hundred and thirty; few and unpleasant have been the years of my life'" (Gen. 47:9). Again, using our math and addition, 1876 plus 130 equals 2006 BC This makes the year of Jacob's birth 2006 BC Isaac, his father, was sixty when he had Jacob: 2006 + 60 = 2066 BC. The year 2066 BC is the year Isaac was born. Abraham was one hundred when he fathered Isaac, making the year of Abram's birth 2166 BC There was 892 years between Abram and Noah, putting the year of Noah's birth at 3058 BC, and there was 1,056 years between Noah and Adam, leaving us with 4114 BC as the year Adam was born.

Birth of Adam		Birth of Noah		Birth of Abraham		Birth of Isaac		Birth of Jacob	Entered Egypt Jacob 130 Yrs	Years In Egypt 430	Exodus	Solomon 4th Yr. Reign
4114BC	1056 Yrs.	3058BC	892 Yrs	2166BC	100 Yrs	2066BC	60 Yrs	2006BC	1876BC		1446BC	966BC

SOLOMON'S REIGN

There is great debate about this timeline because Rameses was not the Pharaoh in 1446 BC However, Ur of the Chaldeans did not exist when Abraham was called by God in Genesis 11:27 either. Scripture is written for us to have an idea of where certain events took place. By stating that Abraham left Ur of the Chaldeans, we can know where that was. Just as Rameses's location and the exodus were known in direct relation to the accounting of a specific location within scriptures, stating that Abraham left Ur of the Chaldeans tells us where that event took place.

The word of God has numbers that have special meaning within Moses's laws, the Gospels, and prophecy. Remember, Jesus did not come to do away with the scripture law of Moses, but rather to fulfill that law (Matt.5:17). The numbers and their meanings are as follows:

One represents absolute singleness and unity (Eph. 4:4–6; John 17:21–22).

Two represents the truth of God's Word; for example, the law and prophets (John 1:45), two or three witnesses (2 Cor. 13:1), and a sword with two edges (Heb. 4:12). See also Mark 6:7 and Revelation 11:3. In the book of Daniel, the number two is used twenty-one times.

Three represents the Godhead or Trinity. The angels cry "holy" three times to the triune God (Isa. 6:3). See also Matthew 28:19 and 1 John 5:7–8.

Four represents universal truth, as in the four directions (north, south, east, west) and four winds (Matt. 24:31; Rev.7:1, 20:8). In Acts 10:11, a sheet with four corners symbolizes the Gospel going to all the gentiles.

Five represents teaching. First, there are the five books of Moses. Second, Jesus talked about the five wise virgins and uses five barley loaves to feed the five thousand.

Six represents the worship of man, and it is the number of man, signifying his rebellion, imperfection, works, and disobedience. It is used 273 times in the Bible, including its derivatives, and another ninety-one times as threescore or sixty. Man was created on the sixth day (Gen. 1:26, 31). See also Exodus 31:15 and Daniel 3:1. The number is especially significant in the book of Revelation, as 666 identifies the beast: "Here is wisdom. Let him that hath understanding count the number of the beast: for it is the number of a man; and his number is Six hundred threescore and six" (Rev. 13:18).

Seven represents perfection and is the sign of God, divine worship, completion, obedience, and rest. See Genesis 2:104, Psalm 119:164, and Exodus 20:8–11 for examples. The number seven is also the most common in biblical prophecy, occurring forty-two times in Daniel and Revelation alone. In Revelation, there are seven churches, seven spirits, seven golden candlesticks, seven stars, seven lamps, seven seals, seven horns, seven eyes, seven angels, seven trumpets, seven thousand slain in a great earthquake, seven heads, seven crowns, seven last plagues, seven golden vails, seven golden vials, seven mountains, and seven kings.

Ten represents law and restoration. Of course, this includes the Ten Commandments found in Exodus chapter 20. See also Matthew 25:1 (ten virgins), Luke 17:17 (ten lepers), and Luke 15:8 (healing).

Twelve represents the church and God's authority. Jesus had twelve disciples, and there were twelve tribes of Israel. In Revelation 12:1, the twenty-four elders and 144,000 are multiples of twelve. The New Jerusalem city has twelve foundations; twelve gates; twelve angels... See Revelation 21.

Forty represents a generation and times of testing. It rained for forty days during the flood. Moses spent forty years in the desert, as did the children of Israel. Jesus fasted for forty days.

Fifty represents power and celebration. The Jubilee came after the forty-ninth year (Exod. 24:10), and the Pentecost occurred fifty days after Christ's resurrection (Acts 2).

Seventy represents human leadership and judgment. Moses appointed seventy elders (Exod. 24:1), and the Sanhedrin was made up of seventy men. Jesus chose seventy disciples (Luke 10:1). Jesus told Peter to forgive seventy times seven.

By using math and history, we can see which prophecies have been fulfilled and which are to come. God does not write scripture without meaning or reason (Rom. 15:4).

CHAPTER 4

DANIEL 2

HISTORY AND PROPHECY FULFILLMENT

After the death of King Solomon, the monarchy was divided into two kingdoms: the northern kingdom of Israel, and the southern kingdom of Judah. Because of the disobedience of God's people, in the year of 722 BC the Assyrians destroyed the northern kingdom, Israel. Then in 538 BC, God sent the Babylonians to the southern kingdom, Judah, who took His people to Babylon. Daniel, one of the many people taken, was trained among the wise men of Babylon.

Nebuchadnezzar was the king of Babylon. He had a dream that troubled him. He called the magicians, astrologers, sorcerers, and the Chaldeans (his wise men) to tell him the meaning of his dream. In addition, he told them that if they could not make known to him his dream and its interpretation, they would be cut into pieces. The Chaldeans told the king that no man on earth could tell the king this matter, only the gods, whose dwelling is not with flesh (Dan. 2:1–11).

Daniel, as one of the wise men, asked the king to give him time so that he might seek God for the answer and tell the king the interpretation. Daniel and his companions sought mercy from God concerning this secret in prayer. God then reveals this secret to Daniel (Dan. 2:16–19).

This dream was about a great image that had a head of gold. Its chest and arms were silver, it's belly and thighs were bronze, and its legs were made of iron. The feet were made partly of iron and partly of clay. A stone, which was cut without hands, struck the image on its feet of iron and clay. It broke the feet into pieces. The feet were crushed together and became like chaff from the summer threshing floors. The wind carried the pieces away so that no trace of them were to be found. The great stone that struck the image became a great mountain and filled the whole earth (Dan. 2:31–35).

This statue is a timeline, and each metal represent a kingdom.

Babylon is the head of gold, which reigned between 605 BC and 539 BC:

> Thou, O king, art a king of kings; for the God of heaven hath given thee a kingdom, power, and strength, and glory. And wheresoever the children of men dwell, the beasts of the field and the fowls of the heaven hat he given into thine hand, and hath made thee ruler over them all. Thou art this head of gold. (Dan. 2:37–38)

Medo-Persia, the chest and arms of silver, conquered Cyrus the Great of Babylon in 539 BC, ruling between 539 BC and 331 BC.

Greece, the belly and thighs of bronze, was conquered by Alexander the Great, who is considered one of the greatest military minds of all time. Their weapons were made of bronze. Greece ruled from 331 B.C to 168 BC.

Rome is the legs of iron. On June 22 in 168 BC, during the Battle of Pydna, Rome became the new great kingdom of iron, reigning between 168 BC and AD 476. This kingdom was in power when Jesus was nailed to the cross.

Diocletian was the first emperor to divide the Roman Empire into the Western Empire and the Eastern Empire in AD 285. In AD 286, Emperor Augustus was given control of the Western Empire. Constantinople was the capital city of Eastern Rome, known as the Latin Empire and the Ottoman Empire.

Eventually the Roman Empire was divided into ten barbarian kingdoms. This was the beginning of the "ten toes" that were part iron and part clay. Those ten toes are symbolic of the barbarian kingdoms.

Historically, the period of the barbarian kingdoms spans between the years AD 409 to AD 910. The ten barbarian kingdoms and their modern-day equivalents are as follows:

- Alemanni—German
- Burgundians—Swiss
- Franks—French
- Lombards—Italian
- Saxons—English
- Suebi—Portuguese
- Visigoths—Spanish
- Heruli—Extinct
- Ostrogoths—Extinct
- Vandals—Extinct

There is only one part of this prophecy and time that remains to be fulfilled. That prophecy at Jesus's Second Coming (the great stone). At this time, the iron mixed with clay will be crushed. God will "set up a kingdom" that "shall never be destroyed." He will restore this world to the original beauty and perfection of Eden and His people to a life of health and happiness:

> And I saw a new heaven and a new earth; for the first heaven and first earth were passed away; and there was no more sea. And I John saw the holy city, new Jerusalem, coming down from God out of heaven, prepared as a bride adorned for her husband. And I heard a great voice out of heaven saying, Behold, the tabernacle of god is with men, and God Himself shall be with them, and be their God. And God shall wipe away all tears from their eyes; and there shall be no more death, neither sorrow, nor crying, neither shall there be any more pain; for the former things are passed away." (Rev. 21:1–4).

PRESENT

From AD 476 to present-day, divided Rome is called Europe. According to Daniel's prophecy, iron and clay would try to unit but would not be successful: "And whereas thou sawest iron mixed with miry clay, they shall mingle themselves with the seed of men: but they shall not cleave one to another, even as iron is not mixed with clay" (Dan. 2:43).

True to prophecy, people throughout history have tried to unit Europe, including the following:

- King Charlemagne of the Franks (AD 768–814)
- King Charles V of Spain (AD 1519–1556)
- Louis XIV of France (AD 1643–1715)
- Napoleon Bonaparte (AD 1804–1814)
- Adolf Hitler (AD 1934–1945)

We cannot stop prophecy. What God declares within prophecy is permanent: "I am the Lord, that is My name; and My glory I will not give to another, nor My praise to carved images. Behold, the former things have come to pass, and new things I declare" (Isa. 42:8–9). "And now I have told you before it comes, that when it does come to pass, you may believe" (John 14:29). We are given prophecy as proof that our Father, the God of Abraham, Isaac, and Jacob, is the only true God, who can declare the future from the beginning.

The prophecies of Daniel were made more than 2,500 years ago, and true to God's word, prophecy has been fulfilled. Daniel interprets Nebuchadnezzar's dream with complete fulfillment:

- Gold/Babylon: BC 605–539
- Silver/Medo Persia: BC 539–331
- Bronze/Greece: BC 331–168
- Iron/Rome: BC 168–476 AD
- Iron and clay/divided Rome and Europe: AD 476–present

UNDERSTANDING IRON MIXED WITH CLAY

Iron, as we have learned, is representative of the Roman Empire. The following scripture gives us the symbolic meaning of clay:

> The word which came to Jeremiah from the Lord, saying: "Arise and go down to the potter's house, and there I will cause you to hear My words." Then I went down to the potter's house, and there he was making something at the wheel. And the vessel that he made of clay was marred in the hand of the potter; so he made it again into another vessel, as it seemed good to the potter to make. Then the word of the Lord came to me, saying: "O house of Israel, can I not do with you as the potter?" says the Lord. "Look, as the clay in the potter's hand, so are you in My hand, O house of Israel." (Jer. 18:1–6)

God forms His church in the way He formed the house of Israel, as a potter's creation with clay.

When God formed Adam in the Garden of Eden in Genesis 2:7, he breaths into his nostrils the "breath of life." The word *breath* here in Hebrew is *Rauh*, meaning soul, mind, or spirit. This is seen in Acts 2:1–4:

> When the Day of Pentecost had fully come, they were all with one accord in one place. And suddenly there came a sound from heaven, as of a rushing wind, and it filled the whole house where they were sitting. Then there appeared to them divided tongues, as of fire, and one sat upon each of them. And they were all filled with the Holy Spirit and began to speak with other tongues, as the Spirit gave them utterance.

The true church of Jesus Christ is those who are filled with the Spirit. Those who have been washed by the precious blood of Jesus and keep His Word, the new Christian church.

The clay mixed with iron is the new Christian church, mixed with the political power of pagan Rome. The term *pagan Rome* comes from their religious system, which was mythology—myths dealing with the gods, demigods, and legends. Paganism, again, began with Nimrod.

In AD 306, Constantine won a series of civil wars. He believed the Christian God helped him win them. History explains that he was given a vision from God and that through the sign of the cross, he would conquer. It was during the reign of Constantine that Christians went from being persecuted to holding positions of governmental influence, including offices in the courts and palaces of kings and as governors.

Because the people in the top tiers of power were now Christians, in order to hold a position of governmental power or to advance in the army, a person was required to become Christian. Intermingling church and state, Constantine made Christianity the religion of state. This brought forth their pagan religion and practices.

Pagan (mythical) statues were renamed as Christian figures. The statue of Jupiter was renamed Peter. The statue of Hermes was renamed Christ the Good Shepard. The statue of Madonna and child was renamed Virgin Mary and baby Jesus.

When Constantine moved his empire to Constantinople in the Eastern Empire, he had to leave someone in charge of the Western Empire. In AD 538, Emperor Justin gave a decree acknowledging the bishop as the head of all churches. That same year, the Roman Church, which had mixed with pagan Rome, was given political, civil, and ecclesiastical power. "Iron mixed with clay," as seen in Daniel's interpretation, symbolizes this union of church and state.

CHAPTER 5

DANIEL 7

HISTORY AND PROPHECY FULFILLMENT

In Daniel 7, we are introduced to four beasts: a lion with eagle's wings, a bear with three ribs in its mouth, a leopard with four wings, and a beast with iron teeth. In Daniel 2, we saw the image of four metals symbolizing the four great world empires from Daniel's day to the end of time. In Daniel 7, we have four beasts that represent the same kingdoms in more detail.

The Lion (Dan. 7:4)

The symbolism of the lion here, again, is Babylon, which took the Israelites captive, as warned by Jeremiah through prophecy:

> Set up the standard toward Zion. Take refuge! Do not delay! For I will bring disaster from the north, and great destruction. The lion has come up from his thicket, and the destroyer of nations is on his way. He has gone forth from his place to make your land desolate. Your cities will be laid waste, without inhabitant. (Jer. 4:6–7)

See also Jeremiah 50:43–44. Daniel goes into more detail about this lion: "I watched till its wings were plucked off; and it was lifted up from the earth and made to stand on two feet like a man, and a man's heart was given to it" (Dan. 7:4b).

God gives King Nebuchadnezzar a touch of humiliation when Nebuchadnezzar declares that great Babylon was built by his own mighty power and not God's. Because of this, Nebuchadnezzar would dwell with beasts and eat grass like oxen for seven years. Through this punishment for his arrogance toward God, Nebuchadnezzar would be taught that the Most High rules (Dan. 4:31–32). After seven years, King Nebuchadnezzar's understanding came back to him and he began to act and think like man again: referred to in Dan. 7:4b: "A man's heart was given to him."

The Bear (Dan. 7:5)

The bear is symbolic of the kingdom of Medo-Persia, whose displayed cruelty and greediness after blood are compared to a bear, which is considered the most voracious and cruel animal. This is parallel in meaning to the breasts and arms of silver seen in Daniel 2: "Raised up on one side" implies that one part of the kingdom would come into greater prominence than the other. Such was the case with Medo-Persian Empire, in which the Persian surpassed the Median. The three ribs have been understood as the conquests before the disappearance of the Babylonians, Lydia (in Turkey), and Egypt. At the height of its power, this empire conquered more than six times as much land as its predecessor, Babylon.

The Leopard (Dan. 7:6)

Medo-Persia was defeated by Macedonian Greece, represented as a leopard with four heads and four wings. The four wings represent unseen swiftness. The conquests of Macedonian Greece under Alexander the Great were more rapid than even those of Babylon. In just three short years, 334–331 BC, he conquered the entire Persian Empire. The leopard is faster and able to think and understand more quickly than a lion or bear, yet it is also more frail. Alexander died in 323 BC at the age of thirty-two. His four strongest generals (Cassandra, Lysimachus, Ptolemy, and Seleucas), divided the kingdom among themselves,—symbolized by the leopard's "four heads".

The Beast (Dan. 7:7)

The previous empires were represented by some of the most ferocious animals of prey, but this beast is represented by a frightful monster. This is a fitting figure of the Roman Empire, which dominated the world with its iron legions. The "iron teeth" of *this* monster give it a direct parallel to the iron in the image painted in Daniel 2:40.

Rome ruled the Mediterranean world when Jesus lived on earth, and it was the Roman governor Pilate who sent Him to the cross, where He died for the sins of all mankind. The ten horns, like the leopard's four heads, show a splintering of the kingdom into multiple parts.

The lion, bear, leopard, and beast were already foretold in the dream of Nebuchadnezzar in Daniel 2. Daniel 7 tells us the ten horns are ten kings (kingdoms, governments, political powers). This beast had ten horns, and another comes up among them, referred to as "another little horn," and three are pulled up by the roots (Dan. 7:7–8). This "little horn" is the Roman Church, which was given political, civil, and ecclesiastical power. The iron mixed with clay is symbolic of the union of church and state.

Three extinct tribes denied the teaching of this corrupted church and state, so the bishop called upon Justinian to get rid of those tribes. Therefore, the ten tribes were now down to seven.

FINAL KINGDOM (DAN. 7:9–10)

In Daniel 2, we saw a stone crush the statue to powder and then fill the earth, vividly portraying the time when these nations will be judged and destroyed. At that time, God will set up His kingdom and reign forever. This chapter adds the fact that God will "sit" for a solemn *day* of judgment before He sets up His "everlasting dominion." His verdict will be both just and merciful because He commits the judgment to His Son, who gave His life for us (John 5:22, 5:37).

In Daniel 7:11–12, this "fourth kingdom" ends in the lake of fire and has no existence beyond:

> And the beast was taken, and with him the false prophet that wrought miracles before him, with which he deceived them that had received the mark of the beast, and them that worshipped him image. These both were cast alive into a lake of fire burning with brimstone. (Rev. 19:20)

CHAPTER 6

THE LITTLE HORN IN DANIEL 7

Daniel 7:20–25 and Revelation 13:1–5 are also seen as parallel:

> And of the ten horns that were in his head, and of the other which came up, and before whom three fell; even of that horn that had eyes and a mouth that spake very great things, whose look was more stout than his fellows. I beheld, and the same horn made war with the saints, and prevailed against them; Until the Ancient of days came, and judgment was given to the saints of the Most High; and the time came that the saints possessed the kingdom. Thus, he said, the fourth beast shall be the fourth kingdom upon earth, which shall be diverse from all kingdoms, and shall devour the whole earth, and shall tread it down, and break it in pieces. And the ten horns out of this kingdom are ten kings that shall arise: and another shall rise after them; and he shall be diverse from the first, and he shall subdue tree kings. And he shall speak great words against the Most High and shall wear out the saints of the most High, and think to change times and laws: and they shall be given into his hand until a time and times and the dividing of times." (Dan. 7:23–25)

And I stood upon the sand of the sea, and saw a beast rise up out of the sea, having seven heads and ten horns, and upon his horns ten crowns, and upon his heads the name of blasphemy. And the beast which I saw was like unto a leopard, and his feet were as the feet of a bear, and his mouth as the mouth of a lion: and the dragon gave him his power, and his seat, and great authority. And I saw one of his heads as it were wounded to death; and his deadly wound was healed: and all the world wondered after the beast. And there was given unto him a mouth speaking great things and blasphemies; and power was given unto him to continue forty and two months. (Rev. 13:1–5)

Symbolically we know that a horn is a king or kingdom: "And the ten horns out of this kingdom are ten kings that shall arise" (Dan. 7:24). Horns are also symbolic for power: "… he had horns coming out of his hand; and there was the hiding of his power" (Hab. 3:4).

This beast we know symbolically to be a kingdom, government, or political power: "These great beasts, which are four, are four kings, which shall arise out of the earth" (Dan. 7:17). The words *king* and *kingdom* are used synonymously in biblical prophecy because you cannot have a king without a kingdom and vice versa. It is the dragon that gives this beast his power. Symbolically the dragon is Satan: "And the great dragon was cast out, that old serpent, called the devil, and Satan, which deceiveth the whole world: he was cast out into the earth, and his angels were cast out with him" (Rev. 12:9).

The ten horns of the beasts, like the feet of iron mixed with clay in Daniel, predicted that the Roman Empire would fragment into ten parts. Barbarian tribes (the ten toes, ten horns, and ten crowns) invaded the empire's territory from the north and east and eventually became the nations of modern Europe.

The beast in Revelation 13 is like the dragon from Revelation 12, as well as Daniel 7 and Daniel 8. They have seven heads and ten horns. The seven heads are seven consecutive kingdoms or governments that

Satan uses to persecute God's faithful church, seen in Revelation 17:10: "And there are seven kings: five are fallen, and one is, and the other is not yet come; and when he cometh, he must continue a short space." Remember that there were ten barbaric kingdoms, but the bishop had Emperor Justin remove three.

We know the dragon to be Satan, while the beast symbolized Satan working in disguise, using a corrupted church to do his work. Revelation 13:5 states that the beast continues for "forty and two months" (the 1,260-year period of the historic iron mixed with clay, papal dominance). In Daniel 7:21, this corrupted church makes "war with the saints," persecuting Christ's true followers who struggled to maintain the truth of God's Word. The beast arose, as predicted, among the populated nations of Europe, symbolized by "the sea" and the "ten horns."

This beast has the characteristics of a leopard, a bear, and a lion, which are the same beastly powers mentioned in Daniel 7; the leopard represents Greece, the bear symbolizes Medo-Persia, and the lion is the symbol for Babylon. This beast represents the historical mixed, corrupted papal church, the same religious and political power portrayed by the little horn of Daniel 7.

The dragon gives this beast "his power, and his seats, and great authority." Pagan Rome gave all these things to the corrupted mixed Roman papacy. It was this corrupted church that Satan used to persecute God's faithful people for hundreds of years. See chapter eight for details.

Revelation 13:1 tells us, "on his heads were blasphemous names." Let us see what God's law says about blasphemy:

> And when they could not come nigh unto him for the press, they uncovered the roof where he was; and when they had broken it up, they let down the bed wherein the sick of the palsy lay. When Jesus saw their faith, he said unto the sick of the palsy, 'Son, thy sins be forgiven thee'. But there were certain of the scribes sitting there, and reasoning in their hearts, why doth this man thus

speaks blasphemies? Who can forgive sins but God only?" (Mark 2:4–7)

According to the law of Moses, which were given to him by God, indicating that one can forgive sins is blasphemy. Only God can forgive sin.

> Jesus answered them, I told you, and ye believed not: the works that I do in my Father's name, they bear witness of me. But ye believe not, because ye are not of my sheep, as I said unto you. My sheep hear my voice, and I know them, and they follow me: and I give unto them eternal life; and they shall never perish, neither shall any man pluck them out of my hand. My Father, which gave them me, is greater than all; and no man is able to pluck them out of my Father's hand. I and my Father are one … Say ye of him, whom the Father hath sanctified, and sent into the world, thou blasphemest; because I said, I am the Son of God?" (John 10:25–30, 36)

According to the law of Moses, which was given to him by God, someone claiming to be God, or the Son of God, is blasphemy.

> And Jesus said, "I am: and ye shall see the Son of Man sitting on the right hand of power, and coming in the clouds of heaven." Then the high priest rent his clothes, and saith, what need we any further witnesses? Ye have heard the blasphemy: what think ye? And they all condemned him to be guilty of death. (Mark 14:60–64)

The beast will speak out against the Most High and wear down the saints of the Highest One, and he will intend to make alterations in time and law, and they will be given into his hand for a time, times, and half a time (Dan. 7:25). Revelation 13:5 reveals the same forty-two months. God's calendar is a 360 day year, however, today the world uses the Roman calendar, a 365 day year.

KEY TO TIME

> Lie thou also upon they left side and lay the iniquity of the house of Israel upon it: according to the number of the days that thou shalt lie upon it thou shalt bear their iniquity. For I have laid upon thee the years of their iniquity, according to the number of the days, three hundred and ninety days: so shalt thou bear the iniquity of the house of Israel. And when thou hast accomplished them, lie again on thy right side, and thou shalt bear the iniquity of the house of Judah forty days: I have appointed thee each day for a year. (Ez. 4:4–6)

> After the number of the days in which ye searched the land, even forty days, *each day for a year*, shall ye bear your iniquities, even forty years, and ye shall know my breach of promise. (Num. 14:34; emphasis mine)

The key to time within prophecy is revealed as follows:

- time = one day or 360 years, per the Jewish year
- times = two days or 720 years, again, per the Jewish year
- half a time = half a day or 180 years.
- time + times + half a time (360 + 720 + 180) = 1260 total years

This corrupted church and state began its rule in AD 538. However, in 1798, Napoleon Bonaparte refused to take orders from this united church and state. He sent his top general, General Berthier, to arrest the pope and claim Rome. He took the power away from the united church and state. The time between Emperor Justin's decree in AD 538 and AD 1798 (when Napoleon Bonaparte refusal to obey the bishop) is 1,260 years. Time, times, and dividing of time.

The united church and state of Rome shed more Christian blood than any other entity that has ever existed on earth. It is said that more than one hundred million Christians were killed during the period called the Holy Inquisition.

CHAPTER 8

HOLY INQUISITION AND THE PROTESTANT REFORMATION

As we dive further into prophecy and history fulfillment, the Holy Inquisition and Protestant Reformation will come into play. Therefore, below is a short review of both.

HOLY INQUISITION

The Holy Inquisition was a permanent institution in the Roman church charged with the eradication of heresy. In the early years of the church, several competing sects called themselves Christian. After Emperor Constantine made Christianity the state religion of the Roman Empire, local administrative structures were pulled together into one hierarchy centered in Rome. Those whose beliefs or practices deviated sufficiently from the orthodoxy of the councils became the objects of efforts to bring them into the fold.

The judge, or inquisitor, could bring suit against anyone. The accused had to testify against him- or herself and did not have the right to face and question his or her accuser. It was acceptable to take testimony from criminals, persons of bad reputation, excommunicated people, and heretics. Sentences could not be appealed. Penalties ranged from imprisonment (usually for life) to death. Death was by burning at the stake.

To even establish an accusation against a bishop required seventy-two witnesses. An accusation against a deacon required twenty-seven witnesses. In cases of nonmembers of the clergy or inferior dignitaries, sadly, two witnesses were sufficient to convict an accused.

PROTESTANT REFORMATION

The Protestant Reformation was a sixteenth-century religious, political, intellectual, and cultural upheaval that splintered Catholic Europe. Reformers like Martin Luther, John Calvin, and Henry VIII challenged papal authority and questioned the Roman Catholic Church's ability to define Christian practice. They argued for a religious and political redistribution of power into the hands of Bible- and pamphlet-reading pastors and princes. The disruption by the Roman Catholic Church triggered wars, persecutions, and the so-called Counter-Reformation. This was the Catholics' delayed yet forceful response to the Protestants.

Historians usually date the start of the Protestant Reformation to the 1517 publication of Martin Luther's *95 Theses*. Its ending can be placed anywhere from the 1555 Peace of Augsburg, which allowed for the coexistence of Catholicism and Lutheranism in Germany, to the 1648 Treaty of Westphalia, which ended the Thirty Years' War. The key ideas of the Protestant Reformation were a call to purify the church and a belief that the Bible, not tradition, should be the sole source of spiritual authority.

In the 1500s, England broke away from the Roman Catholic Church and created a new church called the Church of England. Everyone in England had to belong to this church. A group of people called Separatists wanted to separate from the Church of England. To escape the religious corruption, persecutions, and jurisdiction of the Church of England, the Separatists—under the leadership of William Bradford—decided to leave England for the New World to start a settlement of their own so that they could practice their religion freely. Bradford went to the Virginia Company and asked them for permission to establish a new colony in Virginia. The Virginia Company agreed, so the Pilgrims set sail on the Mayflower in September 1620 to the New World.

It is worth noting that in the name of Christ, Protestants killed thousands of Catholics during this time. By carrying out these killings, they were not practicing what Jesus taught, which is "Judge not, that ye be not judged" (Matt. 7:1).

We must remember this when we witness to others today. If someone does not believe as you do, agree to disagree. This does not mean to hide your light. Please allow your light to shine! It is our duty to spread God's message. After your witness, if someone does not agree with the biblical truth of God's message, walk away; it is now left between them and God.

CHAPTER 9

SEVEN SEALS

SEVEN SEALS WITHIN HISTORY

I would like to make a small note here for the reader. The seals in this chapter reveal the seals throughout history. As our journey continues, these seals will come back to haunt us. History has a way of repeating itself. Scripture is revealed through history (facts), and symbolism. This chapter reveals the historical facts of the seven seals.

Within scripture we have found chapters that parallel with each other. Daniel 2 and Daniel 7 are parallel to Revelation 6.

> Then I saw when the Lamb broke one of the seven seals, and I heard one of the four living creatures saying, as with a voice of thunder, "Come." I looked, and behold, a white horse, and he who sat on it had a bow; and a crown was given to him, and he went out conquering and to conquer. (Rev. 6:12).

It is widely believed by most theologians that this symbolic rider on the white horse is none other than the Antichrist or it's spirit.

> Children, it is the last hour; and just as you heard that antichrist is coming, even now many antichrists have appeared; from this we know that it is the last hour. … Who is the lair but the one who denies that Jesus is the

Christ? This is the antichrist, the one who denies the Father and the Son. (1 John 2:18, 22)

This Antichrist spirit comes "conquering and to conquer." White represents purity and righteousness; however, this rider mimics the pure church, going forth victoriously under the false banner of Jesus. The historic corrupted Roman pagan church, as well as the Holy Inquisition, can both be seen as this rider within our known history, the one who came "conquering and to conquer."

WARS AND RUMORS OF WAR

> When He broke the second seal, I heard a second living creature saying, "Come." And another, a red horse went out; and to him who sat on it, it was granted to take peace from the earth, and that men would slay one another; and a great sword was given to him. (Rev. 6:3–4)

This red horse represents the persecution of the pure church. Red is the color of sin (Isa. 1:18), the dragon (Rev. 12:3), and bloodshed (2 Kings 3:22–23). When the faith and devotion of the church became corrupted, it lost the power of God to carry the Gospel forward in victory. This occurred when the church began using the power of the state, uniting with the dragon (the new church united with pagan Rome). Along with persecution within the church (the Holy Inquisition), the phrase "slay one another" suggests internal controversy, discord, and strife.

> When He broke the third seal, I heard the third living creature saying, "Come." I looked and behold a black horse; and he who set on it had a pair of scales in his hand. And I heard something like a voice in the center of the four living creatures saying, "A quart of wheat for a denarius; and do not damage the oil and the wine." (Rev. 6:5–6)

The color black is darkness and famine. The Bible uses the black horse to represent the corrupted church. Substituting pagan beliefs and practices for the truths of God's Word, the church during this time entered a period of great moral and doctrinal darkness (famine of God's Word). This church caused a scarcity of the Bread of Life (God's Holy Word). As God decreed, "hurt not the oil and wine," which symbolize the Holy Spirit (Zech. 4:3, 6) and the blood of Jesus (Matt. 26:26–29).

Even though the church was in great darkness, God preserved a people with the true Gospel and salvation.

> When He opened the fourth seal, I heard the voice of the fourth living creature saying, "Come and see." So, I looked, and behold, a pale horse. And the name of him who sat on it was Death, and Hades followed with him. And power was given to them over a fourth of the earth, to kill with sword, with hunger, and by beasts of the earth. (Rev. 6:7–8)

Symbolizing a dead church, the pale horse is the color of nausea and death. The church that should have been pointing the way to eternal life was instead spreading death. The spiritual "death" that spread across Christendom was accompanied by a moral and intellectual paralysis. The holy scriptures were forbidden to the people. Nobles, commoners, and clergy alike were largely ignorant of the great truths the scriptures contain. For centuries, the world made no progress in science, arts, or civilization. Millions lived miserable lives of ignorance and squalor. This was known as the Dark Ages.

Ezekiel 14:21 lists war, famine, pestilence, and wild beasts as judgments on apostasy from God. Whenever the church abandons the truth and twists its truth, a famine of God's Word results. Pure Bible truth is replaced with the pestilence of heresy, opening the way for persecutors (wild beasts) to punish and chastise the church, and multitudes perish.

For thus saith the Lord GOD; How much more when I send my four sore judgments upon Jerusalem, the sword, and the famine, and the noisome beast, and the pestilence, to cut off from it man and beast? (Ez. 14:21)

MARTYRS

When the Lamb broke the fifth seal, I saw underneath the altar the souls of those who had been slain because of the Word of God, and because of the testimony which they had maintained; and they cried out with a loud voice, saying, "How long, O Lord, holy and true, will You refrain from judging and avenging our blood on those who dwell on the earth?" And there was given to each of them a white robe; and they were told that they should rest for a little while longer, until the number of their fellow servants and their breather who were to be killed even as they had been, would be complete. (Rev. 6:9–11)

The fifth seal is the martyred church. "Under the altar the souls ... slain for the Word of God." God does not keep literal souls under a literal altar in heaven. During the Middle Ages, the papal system had millions of people put to death because they would not renounce biblical truth (the Holy Inquisition). Here is pictured, in symbolic language, the many martyrs of all ages whose blood, like the blood of Abel (Gen. 4:8–10), cries out to God for justice and vindication of the truths for which they died.

And Cain talked with Abel his brother: and it came to pass, when they were in the field, that Cain rose up against Abel his brother, and slew him. And the LORD said unto Cain, where is Abel thy brother? And he said, I know not: Am I my brother's keeper? And he said, what hast thou done? the voice of thy brother's blood crieth unto me from the ground. (Gen. 4:8–10)

We will be with the Lord at the last trump, when soul and body unit, incorruptible:

> Behold, I shew you a mystery; We shall not all sleep, but we shall all be changed, In a moment, in the twinkling of an eye, at the last trump: for the trumpet shall sound, and the dead shall be raised incorruptible, and we shall be changed. For this corruptible must put on incorruption, and this mortal must put on immortality." (1 Cor. 15:51–53)

END-TIME CHURCH UNTIL THE WRATH OF THE LAMB (SECOND COMING)

> I looked when He broke the sixth seal, and there was a great earthquake; and the sun became black as sackcloth made of hair, and the whole moon became like blood; and the stars of the sky fell to the earth, as a fig tree casts its unripe figs when shaken by a great wind. The sky was split apart like a scroll when it is rolled up, and every mountain and island were moved out of their places. Then the kings of the earth and the great men and the commanders and the rich and the strong and the slave and free man hid themselves in the caves and among the rocks of the mountains; and they said to the mountains and the rocks, "Fall on us and hide us from the presence of Him who sits on the throne, and from the wrath of the Lamb; for the great day of their wrath has come, and who can stand?" (Rev. 6:12–17)

From the mid-1700s until the Second Coming of Christ, the sixth seal is the end-time church. Under the sixth seal, the language shifts from symbolic horses and souls to literal signs and disasters. The prophecy says, "there was a great earthquake"; "the sun became black as sackcloth"; "the moon became as blood"; and "the stars of heaven fell." These signs have all received a striking and impassive fulfillment:

- On November 1, 1755, Lisbon, Portugal, was the center of a tremendous earthquake. Its effects were felt over an area of four million square miles.
- Drawing the dark of night over New England, beginning around nine o'clock in the morning on May 19, 1780, heavy black clouds blotted out the sun. That night, when the darkness finally lessened and the moon appeared, the moon had the appearance of blood.
- November 13, 1833 brought the most extensive display of falling stars that has ever been recorded. These are the same signs that Jesus gave to let us know when His coming would be near.

CHAPTER 10

WARNING OF JUDGMENT

The Roman Empire

Jesus's ministry was during the time when the Roman Empire controlled most of the known world. It was the Roman Empire that crucified Jesus and martyred eleven of His twelve disciples. Apostle John was the only exception.

Emperor Nero horribly targeted Christians for persecution in AD 64. A colossal fire broke out in Rome and destroyed much of the city. Rumors abounded that Nero himself was responsible. However, Nero laid blame on the Christians for angering the gods of Rome. Persecutions included feeding them to the lions in the gladiator arena, burning them at the stake in the arena, beheading them, and using them as lanterns to light the streets of Rome.

In AD 70 it was the Roman Empire that invaded Jerusalem and destroyed God's holy temple. It has been reported that 1,100,000 people were killed. This fact has been disputed, but that does not negate the destruction of God's holy temple and the murder of His people.

As we have learned so far, the persecutions of Christians by the Roman Empire did not stop until AD 306 and Emperor Constantine. Christians went from being persecuted to holding positions of governmental influence, in the courts, and in the palaces of kings and governors, and in AD 538, Emperor Justin gave a decree that acknowledged the bishop as the head of all churches. That same year, the Roman church was given political, civil, and ecclesiastical power. Again, the symbol for this is iron mixed with clay.

Over the last few chapters, we learned about the iron mixed with clay and the little horn in Daniel chapters 2 and 7. Both represent the mixed nature of the historic Roman church and state. Daniel told Nebuchadnezzar in Daniel 2 that God would crush and put an end to all these kingdoms (iron mixed with clay being the last), but His kingdom will be an everlasting kingdom (Dan. 2:44).

THE DESTRUCTION OF ROME

When the seventh seal is broken, the trumpets begin. "When the Lamb broke the seventh seal, there was silence in heaven for about half an hour. And I saw the seven angels who stand before God, and seven trumpets were given to them" (Rev. 8:1–2).

The seven trumpets are a warning to the world of the severe judgments of God. In biblical times, trumpets were used as a call for war.

> And he divided the three hundred men into three companies, and he put a trumpet in every man's hand, with empty pitchers, and lamps within the pitchers. And he said unto them, look on me, and do likewise: and, behold, when I come to the outside of the camp, it shall be that, as I do, so shall ye do. When I blow with a trumpet, I and all that are with me, then blow ye the trumpets also on every side of all the camp, and say, The sword of the Lord, and of Gideon. (Judg. 7:16–18)

Also, the priests blew trumpets to signal the upcoming Day of Atonement, the annual day of judgement (Lev. 23:23–32).

The seven trumpets follow the pattern set by the seven seals, but the trumpets focus on the judgments that God pours out upon the persecutors of His people. They warn of the great day of judgment and retribution, which will end in the utter annihilation of Satan, as well as end sin and all who refuse to repent and separate from their sin (Rev. 20:9–14). The first six trumpets bring partial destruction.

"And the seven angels who had the seven trumpets prepared themselves to sound them" (Rev. 8:8). "Then the angel took the censer and filled it with the fire of the altar and threw it to the earth; and there followed pearls of thunder and sounds and flashes of lightening and a great earthquake" (Rev. 8:5).

This symbolizes God's judgements on the nations. Those who refuse to accept the lesser judgements of the first six trumpets will be destroyed at the seventh trumpet's judgement. The seventh trumpet will sound after everyone has made a final and permanent decision for or against Christ. At this point, intercession for those who have rejected Him will cease, probation will be closed, and every case will be decided (Rev. 22:11).

THE FIRST TRUMPET

> The first sounded, and there came hail and fire mixed with blood, and they were thrown to the earth; and a third of the earth was burned up, and a third of the trees were burned up and all the green grass was burned up. (Rev. 8:7)

Hail and fire mingled with blood symbolize war and bloodshed.

> And I will call for a sword against him throughout all my mountains, saith the Lord God: every man's sword shall be against his brother. And I will bring him to judgment with pestilence and bloodshed; I will rain down on him, on his troops, and on the many peoples who are with him, flooding rain, great hailstones, fire, and brimstone. (Ez. 38:21–22)

The earth, trees, and green grass represent people: "For dust you are, and to dust you shall return" (Gen. 3:19b); "All go to one place: all are from the dust, and all return to dust" (Eccles. 3:20); "The righteous shall flourish like a palm tree, He shall grow like a cedar in Lebanon" (Ps. 92:12); "The field is the world" (Matt. 13:38).

From AD 396 to AD 419, the barbaric Goths from the north fell upon Rome, seen as a plague of "hail" to spill the "blood" of her people and set her proud cities on "fire," headed by their general Alaric. The barbaric Goths sacked and pillaged the city of Rome in AD 410. The term *third part* indicates that a large portion would be affected but not all. In this case, it applies to Rome.

SECOND TRUMPET

> The second angel sounded, and something like a great mountain burning with fire was thrown into the sea; and a third of the sea became blood, and a third of the creatures which were in the sea and had life died; and a third of the ships were destroyed. (Rev. 8:8–9)

Political or religious-political powers are symbolized by the use of a mountain.

> Now it shall come to pass in the latter days that the mountain of the Lord's house shall be established on the top of the mountains and shall be exalted above the hills; and all nations shall flow to it. Many people shall come and say, "Come, and let us go up to the mountain of the Lord, to the house of the God of Jacob; He will teach us His ways, and we shall walk in His paths." For out of Zion shall go forth the law, and the word of the Lord from Jerusalem. (Isa. 2:2–3)

The symbolism also appears in Jeremiah 31:23: "Thus says the Lord of hosts, the God of Israel: 'They shall again use this speech in the land of Judah and in its cities, when I bring back their captivity: The Lord bless you, O home of justice, and the mountain of holiness.'" See also Jeremiah 51:24–25; Ezekiel 17:22–23; and Daniel 2:35, 2:44–45.

People, nations, and tongues are represented by sea or water: "Then he said to me, 'The waters which you saw, where the harlot sits, are peoples, multitudes, nations, and tongues'" (Rev.17:15).

The mountain cast into the sea depicts a violent invasion of a civilized and populated area. The Vandals, led by Genseric, their king, invaded Rome from Africa and the Mediterranean Sea between AD 428 and AD 469. Like a falling mountain thrown into the sea, their sack of Rome in AD 455, which culminated in the unrestrained burning and pillaging of the city, was so dreadful that the word *vandalism* remains to this day as a term for malicious destruction of property.

THIRD TRUMPET

> The third angel sounded, and a great star fell from heaven, burning like a torch, and it fell on a third of the rivers and on the springs of water. The name of the star is called Wormwood; and a third of the waters became wormwood, and many men died from the waters, because they were made bitter. (Rev. 8:10–11)

The third trumpet, the great star that fell from heaven, is symbolic of a great leader or messenger. Wormwood is a bitter plant that is poisonous in large or concentrated doses.

> Now he had still another dream, and related it to his brothers, and said, "Lo, I have had still another dream; and behold, the sun and the moon and eleven stars were bowing down to me." He related it to his father and to his brothers; and his father rebuked him and said to him, "what is this dream that you have had? Shall and your mother and your brothers actually come to

bow ourselves down before you to the ground?" (Gen. 37:9–10)

See also Revelation 1:20 and 22:16.

Attila, ruler of the Huns, was the leader who appeared as a sudden blazing star that brought great bitterness upon Rome. Called the "Scourge of God," Attila called together his hordes of barbarian horsemen, who, without mercy, raped, murdered, pillaged, and turned Roman cities into smoldering ruins. Revelation correctly portrays this invasion as a most bitter judgment.

The Fourth Trumpet

> The fourth angel sounded, and the third of the sun and a third of the moon and a third of the stars were struck, so that a third of them would be darkened and the day would not shine for a third of it, and the night in the same way. (Rev. 8:12)

A third of the sun, moon, and stars are "smitten" with darkness. This represents the removal of Western Rome's leaders. In AD 476, Odoacer, king of the Heruli, deposed Western Roman Emperor Romulus Augustus, bringing an end to the Western Roman Empire. From then on, the Roman united church and state was the dominant figure in Western Europe.

"For the Lord God is a sun and shield; the Lord gives grace and glory; no good thing does He withhold from those who walk upright" (Ps. 84:11) and "But for you who fear My name, the sun of righteousness will rise with healing in wings; and you will go forth and skip about like calves from the stall" (Mal. 4:2). From these two verses, we know that the sun represents God and Jesus. The sun of righteousness was Jesus, who rose with healing on wings. God, Jesus, and the Word are one: "In the beginning was the Word, and the Word was with God, and the Word was God" (John 1:1); "And the Word became flesh, and dwelt among us, and we saw His glory, glory as of the only begotten from the Father, full of grace and truth" (John 1:14).

From the verses above, we can understand that the symbolic meaning of the sun is the Word. The moon reflects the sun, which is symbolic of the church. The stars are symbolic of the messengers of the church.

When the historic pagan Roman church and state took over Western Europe, they darkened the true word, as they had intermingled with the Roman paganism "iron mixed with clay."

> Then I looked, and I heard an eagle flying in mid-heaven, saying with a loud voice, 'Woe, woe, woe to those who dwell on the earth, because of the remaining blasts of the trumpets of the three angel who are about to sound. (Rev. 8:13)

THE FIFTH TRUMPET—FIRST WOE

> Then the fifth angel sounded, and I saw a star from heaven which had fallen to the earth; and the key of the bottomless pit was given to him. He opened the bottomless pit, and smoke went up out of the pit, like the smoke of a great furnace; and the sun and the air were darkened by the smoke of the pit. Then out of the smoke came locusts upon the earth, and power was given them, as the scorpions of the earth, and power was given them, as the scorpions of the earth have power. They were told not to hurt the grass of the earth, nor any green thing, nor any tree, but only men who do not have the seal of God on their foreheads. And they were not permitted to kill anyone, but to torment for five months; and their torment was like the torment of a scorpion when it stings a man. And in those days men

will seek death and will not find it; they will long to die, and death flees from them. (Rev. 9:1–6)

Many Christian commentators, including Martin Luther, the great reformer; Sir Isaac Newton, the famous scientist; and historian Edward Gibbon have seen in the fifth and sixth trumpets the rise and progress of Islam. In the nearly 1,400 since its rise, Islam has had a tremendous impact on the Christian world. In accordance with that truth, the following interpretation deserves serious attention.

As we have seen before, a star represents a leader or messenger. The term *bottomless pit* comes from the Greek word *abyss*, and it means a desolate empty place, similar to the word *void* in Genesis 1:2. This star or great leader was Mohammed, the founder of Islam. The bottomless pit applies here to the vast, desolate wastelands of present-day Saudi Arabia, from which "the smoke" (the religion of Islam) issued forth, darkening the light of Christ and Christianity in all the lands that come under their control.

Out of the smoke comes locusts. When conditions are favorable, a swarm of hundreds of millions of locusts may hatch at the same time. After exhausting the local food supply, they spread out, gobbling up nearly every green plant in their path, leaving desolation and famine behind them. By the time of his death in AD 632, Mohammed had united the Arabian Peninsula under Islam. Over the next one hundred years, the Muslim tide spread in a raging flood across the earth until AD 732, when they were narrowly defeated at the Battle of Tours in France. This victory saved Western Europe from conversion to Islam.

The trees and grass in this scripture set as opposites to "those men which have not the seal of God." The trees and grass represent the many groups of Christians who still preserved the true biblical faith of early Christianity. The locusts were not to hurt these pure commandment-keeping people. The Islamic conquerors did not destroy wantonly or kill Christians and Jews as long as they agreed to pay tribute. They did, however, relentlessly attack the remainder of the Roman Empire, centered in Constantinople, at whom this judgment is directed.

The locusts are given power to "torment" like the sting of a scorpion for five months, or 150 literal years. Starting in 1299 at the Battle of Bapheum, the Turkish Muslims began a persistent assault on the Eastern Roman Empire, or the Byzantine Empire, which became a vassal state subordinate to the Ottoman Empire to outmaneuver the other claimant to the throne and become emperor. During this time period, the Byzantine Empire was "tormented" by the Ottoman Empire but not yet destroyed.

THE SIXTH TRUMPET—THE SECOND WOE

> Then the sixth angel sounded, and I heard a voice from the four horns of the golden altar which is before God, one saying to the sixth angel who had the trumpet, "Release the four angels who are bound at the great river Euphrates." And the four angels, who had been prepared for the hour and day and month and year, were released, so that they would kill a third of mankind. The number of the armies of the horsemen was two hundred million; I heard the number of them. And this is how I saw in the vision the horses and those who sat on them: the riders had breastplates the color of fire and of hyacinth and of brimstone; and the heads of the horses are like the heads of lions; and out of their mouths proceed fire and smoke and brimstone. A third of mankind was killed by these three plagues, by the fire and the smoke and the brimstone which proceeds out of their mouths and in their tails; for their tails are like serpents and have heads, and with them they do harm. (Rev. 9:13–19)

The four angels mentioned in Revelation 7:1 had worldwide power to restrain the winds; in contrast, the present four appear to be localized. These can be viewed as the four sultans of the Turkish Ottoman Empire—Aleppo, Iconium, Damascus, and Baghdad—as destructive forces that moved against western world. These angels had been restrained from their work of judgment until the sixth angel sounded his trumpet.

The Byzantine Empire had been holding the Muslims in check. Now that they were no longer a threat, the Ottoman Empire turned its attention to the Roman church and state dominating Europe—the target of this trumpet's judgment. The Islamic wars played a key role in helping Protestantism thrive by diverting the attention of the Roman church and state persecution long enough to help it become established.

The time set forth here represents 391 years and fifteen days (360 + 30 + 1 + 1/24 of a year), which indicates the time remaining for the Ottoman Empire to do its work. From the end of the fifth trumpet in 1449, 391 years extends to 1840. In that year, the Ottoman Empire could no longer protect itself and accepted the protection of four European nations, effectively ceasing as an independent power.

In ancient times, the cavalry was the swiftest, most mobile branch of the military. The number 200,000,000 is symbolic of a vast, innumerable host. The cavalry was a prominent feature of the Arabian military. The cavalry horsemen's hair, described as "the hair of women," was long and worn under turbans. Pictured on their breastplates of iron were lions. Just as their breastplates depicted, it is written that "they came with the strength and rapacity of lions" and were seemingly unstoppable. The locust wings, like the leopard wings written about in Daniel 7, represent speed. Abaddon in Hebrew and Apollyon in Greek are names that mean "the destroyer."

Fire and brimstone are symbols of judgement (Gen. 19:24). The predominate colors of the Turkish uniforms were red (fire), blue (jacinth and smoke), and yellow (brimstone). Fire and smoke and brimstone from the horses' mouths refer to the use of gunpowder and firearms, which were introduced around this time. "Head of lions" denotes ferocity and majesty. "Their power [authority] was in their mouth and in their tails" perhaps was referring to the Turkish cavalry's guns, speed, mobility, and devious tactics, for which they were widely recognized.

> The rest of mankind, who were not killed by these plagues, did not repent of the works of their hands, so as not to worship demons, and the idols of gold and of silver and of brass and of stone and of wood, which can neither see nor hear nor walk; and they did not repent of their murders nor of their sorceries nor of their immorality nor of their thefts. (Rev. 9:20–21)

After all these judgements, the "represented not" were the rest of the men. God's judgements were not only to punish but also to call the remaining men of the Roman church and state to repentance. The rest of the men are said to worship idols. At this time, the western church worshiped images of saints. The men also did not repent of "their murders" of the Christians slaughtered for their belief in biblical truth. Their "fornication" is a symbol of doctrinal impurity, or of their "thefts," the usurping of God's authority.

CHAPTER 11

THE TWO WITNESSES

HISTORICALLY

During the darkest ages, men have been raised up to testify against the prevailing corruption of their time, especially the corruption of the apostate church. Their opponents have endeavored to silence their voices and blacken their characters, but God has ever vindicated them and given life out of death. Always when the enemies of the truth have deemed themselves triumphant, there has been a rekindling of Gospel testimony.

> And I will give power unto my two witnesses, and they shall prophesy a thousand two hundred and threescore days, clothed in sackcloth. These are the two olive trees, and the two candlesticks standing before the God of the earth. (Rev. 11:3–4)

The two witnesses, which are said to be two olive trees and two candlesticks, here represent the Old and New Testaments. The olive trees represent the power of the Holy Spirit. The candlesticks symbolize the spiritual light of the scriptures. "*Thy word* is a lamp unto my feet, and a light unto my path" (Ps. 119:105; emphasis mine).

> *And two olive trees* by it, one upon the right side of the bowl, and the other upon the left side thereof. So, I

answered and spake to the angel that talked with me, saying, what are these, my lord? Then the angel that talked with me answered and said unto me, Knowest thou not what these be? And I said, No, my lord. Then he answered and spake unto me, saying, *this is the word of the Lord* unto Zerubbabel, saying, Not by might, nor by power, but by my spirit, saith the LORD of hosts." (Zech. 4:3–6; emphasis mine)

The two witnesses were to prophesy in sackcloth, symbolizing mourning. The Bible was not readily available to the common people. There are several reasons for this:

1. It was only available in Hebrew, Greek, and Latin.
2. It had to be copied by hand, so there were few copies.
3. During the religious services, both scripture reading and sermons were in Latin.
4. The church's stance was that since the common people could not understand the Bible, the clergy must interpret it for them.
5. Even after the Bible was translated into the common language of the people, the church forbade them to read it.

And if any man will hurt them, fire proceedeth out of their mouth, and devoureth their enemies: and if any man will hurt them, he must in this manner be killed. These have power to shut heaven, that it rain not in the days of their prophecy: and have power over waters to turn them to blood, and to smite the earth with all plagues, as often as they will. (Rev. 11:5–6)

There is a penalty for the misrepresenting biblical truths and teaching error: "For I testify unto every man that heareth the words of the prophecy of this book, if any man shall add unto these things, God shall add unto him the plagues that are written in this book" (Rev. 22:18). The two witnesses are represented as bringing some Old

Testament style punishment upon those who "hurt" the scriptures by their false teachings. Medieval Europe suffered terribly from wars, famines, and disease that killed millions of people because of the church's rejection of the scriptures.

> And when they shall have finished their testimony, the beast that ascendeth out of the bottomless pit shall make war against them, and shall overcome them, and kill them. And their dead bodies shall lie in the street of the great city, which spiritually is called Sodom and Egypt, where also our Lord was crucified. And they of the people and kindreds and tongues and nations shall see their dead bodies three days and an half, and shall not suffer their dead bodies to be put in graves. And they that dwell upon the earth shall rejoice over them, and make merry, and shall send gifts one to another; because these two prophets tormented them that dwelt on the earth. (Rev. 11:7–10)

At the end of the 1,260 years, when the two witnesses have finished prophesying "clothed in sackcloth," the beast comes out of the bottomless pit to make war against them and kill them. The excesses and corruption of the corrupted papal church system and church-supported aristocracy got so bad that their firmest supporter, France, became their worst enemy. This nation not only rejected Catholicism but God Himself; they cast out all morals and everything Christian and set up a new religion glorifying man, reason, and intellect of gods.

During the Reign of Terror in France, the Bible was not only openly rejected but also forbidden and publicly burned. For "three days and a half" (symbolizing three and a half years), the Bible would appear to be "dead." For three and a half years, the revolutionaries of France did all in their power to oppose and destroy the Bible.

> And after three days and a half the Spirit of life from God entered into them, and they stood upon their feet;

and great fear fell upon them which saw them. And
they heard a great voice from heaven saying unto them,
Come up hither. And they ascended up to heaven in a
cloud; and their enemies beheld them. (Rev. 11:11–12)

The scene here is of the two witnesses as they are given new "life"
and exalted in the sight of their enemies. After the French Revolution,
protestant Europe looked back on its extremes with disgust and sought
with fervent effort to elevate the Bible to greater prominence than
ever. The British Bible Society, established in 1804, and American
Bible Society, established in 1816, began distributing large numbers
of Bibles. In 1804, the total number of Bibles in circulation was about
four million in more than fifty languages. Today there are billions of
Bibles in hundreds of languages, making it the world's most widely
circulated book.

And the same hour was there a great earthquake, and
the tenth part of the city fell, and in the earthquake
were slain of men seven thousand: and the remnant
were affrighted and gave glory to the God of heaven.
(Rev. 11:13)

The French Revolution and the empire that followed it under
Napoleon Bonaparte left Europe in shambles.

CHAPTER 12

THE TWO WITNESSES

TODAY

> And I will give power unto my two witnesses, and they
> shall prophesy a thousand two hundred and threescore
> days, clothed in sackcloth. These are the two olive trees,
> and the two candlesticks standing before the God of the
> earth. (Rev. 11:3–4)

THE OLIVE TREE

> And two olive trees by it, one upon the right side of
> the bowl, and the other upon the left side thereof. So,
> I answered and spake to the angel that talked with me,
> saying, what are these, my lord? Then the angel that
> talked with me answered and said unto me, Knowest
> thou not what these be? And I said, No, my lord. Then
> he answered and spake unto me, saying, this is the word
> of the Lord unto Zerubbabel, saying, Not by might,
> nor by power, but by my spirit, saith the Lord of hosts.
> (Zech. 3:2–6)

Here in Zechariah, we have been shown the two olive trees as the Word
of God. The Word of God was given initially to the descendants of

Abraham, the Israelites. The Lord called the Israelites "a green olive tree":

> The Lord called thy name, A green olive tree, fair, and of goodly fruit: with the noise of a great tumult he hath kindled fire upon it, and the branches of it are broken. For the Lord of hosts, that planted thee, hath pronounced evil against thee, for the evil of the house of Israel and of the house of Judah, which they have done against themselves to provoke me to anger in offering incense unto Baal. (Jer.11:16–17)

Symbolically the olive tree represents the Word, the Israelites, and then the Gentiles. When Jesus came into the world, the Word became flesh. Because of the disbelief of the Jewish people, God gave His message (the Word) to the Gentiles to be "grafted into" the olive tree. "For I am not ashamed of the gospel of Christ: for it is the power of God unto salvation to everyone that believeth; to the Jew first, and also to the Greek" (Rom. 1:16).

> And if some of the branches be broken off, and thou, being a wild olive tree, wert graffed in among them, and with them partakest of the root and fatness of the olive tree; Boast not against the branches. But if thou boast, thou bearest not the root, but the root thee. Thou wilt say then, the branches were broken off, that I might be grafted in. (Rom. 11:17–19)

The Gentiles are adopted into the family of Abraham by the blood of Jesus. "But when the fullness of time come, God sent forth His Son, made of a woman, made under the law, To redeem them that were under the law, that we might receive the adoption of sons" (Gal. 4:3–4)—a "wild olive tree."

Today, the two olive trees represent first the Jewish children of God who were saved by Jesus Christ and, second, the Gentiles, described as "a wild branch grafted into the family" by the blood of Jesus.

THE TWO CANDLESTICKS

> And I turned to see the voice that spake with me. And being turned, I saw seven *golden candlesticks;* And in the midst of the seven candlesticks one like unto the Son of man, clothed with a garment down to the foot, and girt about the paps with a golden girdle. (Rev. 1:12–13; emphasis mine)

Here John sees a vision of Jesus holding seven golden candlesticks. In Revelation 1:20, John tells us exactly what the seven candlesticks represent: "The mystery of the seven stars which thou sawest in my right hand, and the seven golden candlesticks. The seven stars are the angels of the seven churches: and the seven candlesticks which thou sawest are the seven churches."

These seven churches represent the churches of today, first the Jewish believers and then His Gentile believers. Two groups of people give witness of Jesus Christ:

1. Israelites: "Ye are my witnesses, saith the LORD, and my servant whom I have chosen: that ye may know and believe me, and understand that I am he: before me there was no God formed, neither shall there be after me" (Isa. 43:10); "Fear ye not, neither be afraid: have not I told thee from that time and have declared it? ye are even my witnesses. Is there a God beside me? yea, there is no God; I know not any" (Isa. 44:8).

2. Gentiles: "But ye shall receive power, after that the Holy Ghost is come upon you: and ye shall be witnesses unto me both in Jerusalem, and in all Judaea, and in Samaria, and unto the uttermost part of the earth" (Acts 1:8); "And I will give power

unto my two witnesses, and they shall prophesy a thousand two hundred and threescore days, clothed in sackcloth" (Rev. 11:3).

Peter tells us that in the last days, Jesus will pour out His Spirit on His people, both the believing Israelites and Gentiles:

> And it shall come to pass in the last days, saith God, I will pour out of my Spirit upon all flesh: and your sons and your daughters shall prophesy, and your young men shall see visions, and your old men shall dream dreams: And on my servants and on my handmaidens I will pour out in those days of my Spirit; and they shall prophesy: And I will shew wonders in heaven above, and signs in the earth beneath; blood, and fire, and vapour of smoke." (Acts 2:17–19)

My friends, if you have accepted Jesus as your personal Savior, then you are one of these witnesses.

CHAPTER 13

THE 144,000

And I saw another angel ascending from the east, having the seal of the living God: and he cried with a loud voice to the four angels, to whom it was given to hurt the earth and the sea, Saying, Hurt not the earth, neither the sea, nor the trees, till we have sealed the servants of our God in their foreheads. And I heard the number of them which were sealed: and there were sealed an hundred and forty and four thousand of all the tribes of the children of Israel. Of the tribe of Judah were sealed twelve thousand. Of the tribe of Reuben were sealed twelve thousand. Of the tribe of Gad were sealed twelve thousand. Of the tribe of Asher were sealed twelve thousand. Of the tribe of Naphtali were sealed twelve thousand. Of the tribe of Manasseh were sealed twelve thousand. Of the tribe of Simeon were sealed twelve thousand. Of the tribe of Levi were sealed twelve thousand. Of the tribe of Issachar were sealed twelve thousand. Of the tribe of Zebulun were sealed twelve thousand. Of the tribe of Joseph were sealed twelve thousand. Of the tribe of Benjamin were sealed twelve thousand." (Rev. 7:2–8)

After the death of King Solomon, the monarchy split into the northern kingdom of Israel and the southern kingdom of Judah. The kingdom of the north was destroyed by the Assyrians in 722 BC: "In the ninth year of Hoshea the king of Assyria took Samaria, and carried Israel away into Assyria, and placed them in Halah and in Habor by the river of Gozan, and in the cities of Medes" (2 Kings 17:6).

Because the tribe of the north intermingled with the Assyrians, there are very few of their true Jewish linage left.

The southern kingdom of Judah was captured by Babylon in 586 BC. However, in 516 BC, the southern kingdom of Judah could return to Jerusalem. The southern kingdom of the tribes of Judah, Benjamin, and Levi returned and still have true linages.

It is my opinion, as well as that of other theologians, that these are not literal Jews but spiritual ones because of the lack of true Israelites left from the northern kingdom.

"And if ye be Christ's, then are ye Abraham's seed, and heirs according to the promise" (Gal. 3:29). Gentiles (anyone not of Jewish descent) are considered Abraham's seed by adoption. The precious blood of Jesus gives us our birthright:

> For he is not a Jew, which is one outwardly; neither is that circumcision, which is outward in the flesh: But he is a Jew, which is one inwardly; and circumcision is that of the heart, in the spirit, and not in the letter; whose praise is not of men, but of God. (Rom. 2:28)

When Jacob (Israel) had his children, they were given names with special meanings:

1. Judah—"I will praise the Lord"
2. Reuben—"He has looked on me"
3. Gad—"Given good fortune"
4. Asher—"Happy am I"
5. Naphtali—"My wrestling"
6. Manasseh—"Making me to forget"
7. Simeon—"God hears me"
8. Levi—"Attached to me"
9. Issachar—"Purchased me"
10. Zebulun—"Dwelling"
11. Joseph—"God will add me"
12. Benjamin—"Son of His right hand"

Now let us put these meanings together and see what they mean as one: "I will praise the Lord for He has looked on me and granted good fortune. I am happy because my wrestling. God is making me to forget. God hears me and is attached to me. He has purchased me a dwelling and will add to me the Son of His right hand." This is the story of salvation.

The modern-day apostles who follow the teachings of Jesus are considered witnesses and a part of the 144,000. Furthermore, in Acts 1, after Judas Iscariot betrayed Jesus and hung himself, Peter stood up among the apostles and told them they must replace him to complete the twelve. In the next chapter, the twelve apostles were all filled with the Holy Spirit, as well as 120 in the upper room simultaneously: "And in those days, Peter stood up in the midst of the disciples, and said, (the number of names together were about an hundred and twenty)" (Acts 1:15).

Three thousand were converted as a result of the Holy Spirit.

CHAPTER 14

THE MARK (OR SEAL)

"And I heard the number of them which were sealed: and there were sealed an hundred and forty and four thousand of all the tribes of the children of Israel" (Rev. 7:4).

SYMBOLIC

The 144,000 have a name and a seal in their foreheads, which are representative of your thoughts of worship and obedience to God's will. If you are doing the will of God, it will show in your actions, representative of "thine hand": "And thou shalt bind them for a sign upon thine hand, and they shall be as frontlets between thine eyes" (Deut. 6:8).

"And the LORD said unto him, 'Go through the midst of the city, through the midst of Jerusalem, and set a mark upon the foreheads of the men that sigh and that cry for all the abominations that be done in the midst thereof'" (Ez. 9:4). The idolators were killed, however; God set a seal on those who repented. But those who had no mark, were slain.

Ephesians 4:30 explains what the seal is: "And grieve not the holy Spirit of God, whereby ye are sealed unto the day of redemption." Seal the Law in my people's heart, "Bind up the testimony, seal the law among my disciples."

The seal is found in the heart of His law, the Word, Jesus, and the

Holy Spirit. A seal has the name, the title, and the territory to whom they belong, such as the seal of the Queen of British Columbia.

The symbolic seal of God is as follows: Jesus is the King of Salvation (the Son of God), and His territory is the kingdom of heaven, to whom we belong.

This mark of the beast physically has yet to happen. As we get into the next chapter and learn about the "beast with two horns," we will have more of an idea of what this mark may be.

CHAPTER 15

THE BEAST WITH TWO HORNS LIKE A LAMB

"And I beheld another beast coming up out of the earth; and he had two horns like a lamb, and he spake as a dragon" (Rev. 13:11).

The beast in the vision comes up "out of the earth" and is described as having two horns like a lamb. Five clues help to accurately determine its identity. With these five clues, we can see that the beast is none other than the United States, as you will notice with our own history:

1. The United States comes to power around 1798 as the historic corrupted papal church is going into captivity and receiving its deadly wound. At that time, the US was just "coming up" as a youthful nation. The US declared its independence on July 4, 1776, and by 1790, all thirteen colonies had ratified the Constitution. This nation was quickly drawn into world politics and today is a world superpower.

2. The "sea" represents multitudes and nations (Rev. 17:15). The beasts that arise from the sea usually do so amid the strife of war. By contrast, this one comes out of the earth, representing a relatively peaceful emergence in a comparatively unpopulated area. This is exactly the way the US came to power.

3. This beast with two horns like a lamb represents a nation of youth, innocence, and gentleness, which is based on the two great principles of civil and religious liberty, "for where the spirit

of the Lord is there is liberty" (2 Cor. 3:17). At its inception, the US had the strength of its form of government and of its people's religion. Republicanism and Protestantism were the fundamental principles of the nation. These principles are the secret of its power and prosperity. It is strong because the government and the church are separate, without one controlling the other.

4. It is noteworthy that this beast lacks any crowns. The US is a grand experiment in government that serves its people rather than enslaving them. A government that allows freedom of conscience and expression. It is a country that has government without a king and religion without a pope.

5. It is this world power that is strong enough to force the world, upon pain of death, to worship the image of the beast:

And he exerciseth all the power of the first beast before him, and causeth the earth and them which dwell therein to worship the first beast, whose deadly wound was healed. And he doeth great wonders, so that he maketh fire come down from heaven on the earth in the sight of men, And deceiveth them that dwell on the earth by the means of those miracles which he had power to do in the sight of the beast; saying to them that dwell on the earth, that they should make an image to the beast, which had the wound by a sword, and did live. And he had power to give life unto the image of the beast, that the image of the beast should both speak, and cause that as many as would not worship the image of the beast should be killed. And he causeth all, both small and great, rich and poor, free and bond, to receive a mark in their right hand, or in their foreheads: And that no man might buy or sell, save he that had the mark, or the name of the beast, or the number of his name. (Rev. 13:12–17)

This beast will speak "as a dragon" and exercise "all power of the first beast before him." Society will become evil and violent, and this Protestant America will demand that the government enforce religious laws. As we have seen in our previous prophecy and history, this happened when the church intermingled with the state of the Roman Empire, creating a corrupted church.

It grieves me to see our government slowly taking this direction, as it has become more and more involved in how we worship and has created laws that go against God's Word:

1. *Engel v. Vitale*, 1962 (prayer taken out of schools)
2. *Abington School District v. Schempp*, 1963 (removal of Bible reading in schools)
3. *Roe v. Wade*, 1973 (legalization of abortion)
4. *United States v. Windsor*, 2013 (legalization of same-sex marriages)

As the world conditions continue to deteriorate, economic sanctions will be legislated against those who refuse to comply, and they will be unable to buy or sell. Finally, a death decree will be issued against them. In order to buy and sell, people will have to have a unique mark. While this mark is unknown, several types of marks have been suggested. In the past, some believed the mark to be our Social Security numbers. Then it was suggested that online banking was the mark. Tattoos were also considered the mark. Today some believe it will be a new chip implanted under our skin. Whatever this mark may be, I am sure as Christians we will know its source and meaning.

CHAPTER 16

ABOMINATION OF DESOLATION

Daniel 11 and 12

DANIEL 11

The language of Daniel 11 and 12 is not symbolic in the same way it is in chapters 2, 7, and 8. There are no images, beasts, or horns. Just the same, its language is cryptic, almost like a code. Each sentence condenses quantities of information, and many metaphors are employed.

These qualities have led to a variety of interpretations. There are, however, two very useful guidelines that all interpretations must follow to be acceptable:

1. This vision begins with a reference to King Cyrus and ends with God's people delivered. So just like the other prophecies of Daniel, this one does not focus on a narrow span of history but instead covers a long span from the prophet's day to the end of the world. This also means there should be some parallels that can be identified between this vision and the previous ones.
2. Within the text are several specific phrases that can be accurately pinned to certain historical events or time periods.

Take, for example, Daniel 11:2: "And now will I shew thee the truth.

Behold, there shall stand up yet three kings in Persia; and the fourth shall be far richer than they all: and by his strength through his riches he shall stir up all against the realm of Grecia." The fourth king of Persia after Cyrus was Xerxes (Greek name for Ahasuerus), the husband of Queen Esther, who ruled at the height of Persian power and wealth. He raised a huge army with contingents from forty different nations and attacked Greece around 480 BC.

The Persian invasion was eventually repelled, but it roused a burning desire on the part of the independent city states of Greece to unite and avenge themselves against the Persians. There is much more detail on the rulers and activities of this kingdom than we have seen in previous visions.

> And a mighty king shall stand up, that shall rule with great dominion, and do according to his will. And when he shall stand up, his kingdom shall be broken, and shall be divided toward the four winds of heaven; and not to his posterity, nor according to his dominion which he ruled: for his kingdom shall be plucked up, even for others beside those. (Dan. 11:3–4)

Daniel 11:3–4 deal with Alexander's conquests and the subsequent four divisions of his kingdom. This is the end of the obvious and easy sections of this prophecy.

> And the king of the south shall be strong, and one of his princes; and he shall be strong above him and have dominion; his dominion shall be a great dominion. And in the end of years they shall join themselves together; for the king's daughter of the south shall come to the king of the north to make an agreement: but she shall not retain the power of the arm; neither shall he stand, nor his arm: but she shall be given up, and they that brought her, and he that begat her, and he that strengthened her in these times. But out of a branch of

her roots shall one stand up in his estate, which shall come with an army, and shall enter into the fortress of the king of the north, and shall deal against them, and shall prevail: And shall also carry captives into Egypt their gods, with their princes, and with their precious vessels of silver and of gold; and he shall continue more years than the king of the north. So, the king of the south shall come into his kingdom and shall return into his own land. But his sons shall be stirred up and shall assemble a multitude of great forces: and one shall certainly come, and overflow, and pass through then shall he return, and be stirred up, even to his fortress. And the king of the south shall be moved with choler, and shall come forth and fight with him, even with the king of the north: and he shall set forth a great multitude; but the multitude shall be given into his hand. And when he hath taken away the multitude, his heart shall be lifted up; and he shall cast down many ten thousand: but he shall not be strengthened by it. For the king of the north shall return and shall set forth a multitude greater than the former and shall certainly come after certain years with a great army and with much riches. And in those times, there shall many stand up against the king of the south: also, the robbers of thy people shall exalt themselves to establish the vision; but they shall fall. So, the king of the north shall come, and cast up a mount, and take the most fenced cities: and the arms of the south shall not withstand, neither his chosen people, neither shall there be any strength to withstand. (Dan.11:5–15)

Daniel 11:5–15 deals with the details of the rulers and activities of the divided kingdom of Greece. Ultimately, two of these divisions came to dominate to such an extent that the Bible record accurately portrays them under the titles of the "king of the north" and the "king of the south."

The enemies of Israel, such as Babylon and Egypt, always attacked from the north and the south. Thus, the "king of the north" and the "king of the south" came to symbolize the adversaries of God's people. This entire vision depicts these enemies as warring powers whose battles adversely affect God's people.

> But he that cometh against him shall do according to his own will, and none shall stand before him: and he shall stand in the glorious land, which by his hand shall be consumed. He shall also set his face to enter with the strength of his whole kingdom, and upright ones with him; thus shall he do: and he shall give him the daughter of women, corrupting her: but she shall not stand on his side, neither be for him. After this shall he turn his face unto the isles and shall take many: but a prince for his own behalf shall cause the reproach offered by him to cease; without his own reproach he shall cause it to turn upon him. Then he shall turn his face toward the fort of his own land: but he shall stumble and fall, and not be found. Then shall stand up in his estate a raiser of taxes in the glory of the kingdom: but within few days he shall be destroyed, neither in anger, nor in battle. (Dan. 11:16–20)

Daniel 11:16–20 applies to the Roman Empire; it is the "king of the north" that "none shall stand before." In 62 BC, the Roman General Pompey interceded in a Jewish civil war and declared Judaea a Roman protectorate.

Verses 17–19 are generally applied to Julius Caesar, ending with his assassination. Caesar Augustus, who at the time of Christ's birth decreed that "the entire world should be taxed" (Luke 2:1), is pointed out in verse 20.

And with the arms of a flood shall they be overflown from before him, and shall be broken; yea, also the prince of the covenant. And after the league made with him he shall work deceitfully: for he shall come up, and shall become strong with a small people. (Dan. 11:22–23)

Daniel 11:22–23 is still the Roman Empire, referring to its power's part in the death of Christ. Verse 23 shifts to the historic corrupted Roman church and state, who magnified himself even to the prince of the host in Daniel 8:11: "Yea, he magnified himself even to the prince of the host, and by him the daily sacrifice was taken away, and the place of his sanctuary was cast down."

And he shall stir up his power and his courage against the king of the south with a great army; and the king of the south shall be stirred up to battle with a very great and mighty army; but he shall not stand: for they shall forecast devices against him. Yea, they that feed of the portion of his meat shall destroy him, and his army shall overflow, and many shall fall down slain. And both these kings' hearts shall be to do mischief, and they shall speak lies at one table; but it shall not prosper: for yet the end shall be at the time appointed. Then shall he return into his land with great riches; and his heart shall be against the holy covenant; and he shall do exploits and return to his own land. At the time appointed he shall return and come toward the south; but it shall not be as the former, or as the latter. For the ships of Chittim shall come against him: therefore, he shall be grieved, and return, and have indignation against the holy covenant: so, shall he do; he shall even return, and have intelligence with them that forsake the holy covenant. (Dan.11:25–30).

Two different historical events could fit the interpretation of Daniel 11:25–30. The first refers to the civil war between the Roman Empire, ruled by Octavian Augustus, the "king of the north" in conflict with Mark Antony and Cleopatra in Egypt, the "king of the south," in 31 BC. The second and most logical to the verses before refers to the crusades of the corrupted mixed Roman church and state as the "king of the north" who launched to reclaim the Holy Land from the Muslims, the "king of the south," around AD 1095–1272.

> And arms shall stand on his part, and they shall pollute the sanctuary of strength, and shall take away the daily sacrifice, and they shall place the abomination that maketh desolate. And such as do wickedly against the covenant shall he corrupt by flatteries: but the people that do know their God shall be strong and do exploits. And they that understand among the people shall instruct many: yet they shall fall by the sword, and by flame, by captivity, and by spoil, many days. Now when they shall fall, they shall be holpen with a little help: but many shall cleave to them with flatteries. And some of them of understanding shall fall, to try them, and to purge, and to make them white, even to the time of the end: because it is yet for a time appointed. (Dan. 11:31–35)

In Daniel 11:31–35, "the abomination that maketh desolate" refers to the historic mixed church and state, the Reformation period, and the persecution of the "heretics" by the Roman Catholic papacy. "Even to the time of the end" refers to the same mixed message of God's Word, as it will be similar to the corrupt church and state, truth mixed with traditions. Furthermore, the end-time church will want their "ears tickled" by a truth that fits their lifestyle (2 Tim. 4:3).

> And the king shall do according to his will; and he shall exalt himself, and magnify himself above every

god, and shall speak marvelous things against the God of gods and shall prosper till the indignation be accomplished: for that that is determined shall be done. Neither shall he regard the God of his fathers, nor the desire of women, nor regard any god: for he shall magnify himself above all. But in his estate shall he honor the God of forces: and a god whom his fathers knew not shall he honor with gold, and silver, and with precious stones, and pleasant things. Thus shall he do in the most strong holds with a strange god, whom he shall acknowledge and increase with glory: and he shall cause them to rule over many, and shall divide the land for gain. (Dan. 11:36–39)

Daniel 11:36–39 parallels closely the description of the "little horn" in Daniel 7 and 8, which we have already studied.

And at that time of the end shall the king of the south push at him: and the king of the north shall come against him like a whirlwind, with chariots, and with horsemen, and with many ships; and he shall enter into the countries, and shall overflow and pass over. He shall enter also into the glorious land, and many countries shall be overthrown: but these shall escape out of his hand, even Edom, and Moab, and the chief of the children of Ammon. He shall stretch forth his hand also upon the countries: and the land of Egypt shall not escape. But he shall have power over the treasures of gold and of silver, and over all the precious things of Egypt: and the Libyans and the Ethiopians shall be at his steps. But tidings out of the east and out of the north shall trouble him: therefore he shall go forth with great fury to destroy, and utterly to take away many. And he shall plant the tabernacles of his palace between the seas

in the glorious mountain; yet he shall come to his end,
and none shall help him.

Daniel 11:40–45 are current to end-of-days events. Some scholars
believe these to be the radical Muslim movement, as tiding from the
east is referred to in verse 44. We have seen this movement already with
the known ISIS attacks.

Verse 45 refers to the Dome of the Rock, which sits where God's
Holy Temple should be, and it will meet its end. It is in the holy place
and has taken away sacrifices because the Jewish state of Israel is not
allowed to rebuild their temple.

DANIEL 12

> And from the time that the daily sacrifice shall be taken
> away, and the abomination that maketh desolate set up,
> there shall be a thousand two hundred and ninety days.
> Blessed is he that waiteth, and cometh to the thousand
> three hundred and five and thirty days. But go thou thy
> way till the end be: for thou shalt rest and stand in thy
> lot at the end of the days. (Dan. 12:11–13)

The 1,290 days begins when the daily sacrifice is taken away and
the "abomination that maketh desolate" is set up. In this text the
abomination that is set up is the historic church-and-state religious
system. The best explanation is that this time period starts in AD 508.
At this time, the question of supremacy between the Catholic and Arian
branches of Christianity was settled in favor of Catholicism by the
subjection of the Arian tribes by Clovis, king of the Franks.

Using the "day for a year rule" makes the 1,290 days end in AD
1798. If we start the 1,335 days at the same time, it brings us up to 1843,
extremely near the end of the 2,300 days/years of Daniel 8:14: "And he
said unto me, Unto two thousand and three hundred days; then shall
the sanctuary be cleansed."

THE DEADLY WOUND

The iron mixed with clay church and state of the Middle Ages ended in the year 1798, exactly 1,260 years after Justinian's decree established the papacy as the supreme Christian power in AD 538. In 1798, Napoleon's army took the pope captive and put him into exile. The murder of a Frenchman in Rome in 1798 gave the French the excuse they wanted to occupy the Eternal City.

It was believed that the era of the church and state had come to an end forever. However, the prophecy says, "and his deadly wound was healed, and all the world wondered after the beast" (Rev. 13:3).

Since the church and state lost its political status after the pope's capture in 1798, it was, for all intents and purposes, dead. It could only be resurrected if it regained its political status.

In 1929, Italian Prime Minister Benito Mussolini and Cardinal Pietro Gasparri signed an accord whereby the pope had to pledge his own political party's support to Mussolini in exchange for the return of his papal seat and power. This monumental event was recorded in the *San Francisco Chronicle* with the heading "Mussolini and Gasparri sign Historic Roman Pact." Even at that point, people understood the significance of what had happened. From 1929 onward, the political status of the Vatican was thus reinstated and the wound could heal fully.

This does not mean that I believe the Roman Catholic Church today is the beast or Antichrist spirit. It does, however, have some of the same characteristics. As do other churches that have their hands in the political arena and who have mingled biblical truth with their own agendas, lies, and deceptions.

CHAPTER 17

PARABLE OF THE FIG TREE

Speaking with his disciples about *when* his Second Coming would take place, Jesus said:

> Now learn a parable of the fig tree; When his branch is yet tender, and putteth forth leaves, ye know that summer is nigh: So likewise ye, when ye shall see all these things, know that it is near, even at the doors. Verily I say unto you, this generation shall not pass, till all these things be fulfilled." (Matt. 24:32–33)

What is this about? What generation shall not pass away before Jesus returns? The answer is in Jesus's parable. It is the generation that sees the fig tree put forth its leaves! In parables, one thing always represents other things. As in Jesus's parable of the sower, the seed represented the Word of God. Similarly, in his parable of the tares, the tares represented the "children of the wicked one" (Matt. 13:38).

The fig tree is clearly represented in the Bible as the nation of Israel: "I found Israel like grapes in the wilderness; I saw your fathers as the first fruits in the *fig tree* at her first time: but they went to Baalpeor and separated themselves unto that shame; and their abominations were according as they loved" (Hos 9:10; emphasis mine).

Jesus was saying in his parable of the fig tree that (I am paraphrasing) "The generation of people that is born on earth the same year the nation of Israel comes back on the map again will not all pass away (die) before my Second Coming occurs." What is even more amazing about this parable is the fact that when Jesus uttered it, Israel was still a nation of people. They were just under Rome's control. In other words, through this parable, Jesus was also prophesying the destruction of the nation of Israel! As prophesied, this happened. Stunningly and amazingly, the nation of Israel came back on the map in 1948. The beginning of Israel coming back on the map started with the Balfour Declaration in 1917.

THE BALFOUR DECLARATION

The Balfour Declaration was a November 2, 1917 letter from British Foreign Secretary Arthur James Balfour to Lord Rothschild that made public the British support of a Jewish homeland in Palestine. The Balfour Declaration led the League of Nations to entrust the United Kingdom with the Palestine Mandate in 1922.

On May 14, 1948, David Ben-Gurion, the head of the Jewish Agency, proclaimed the establishment of the State of Israel. US President Harry S. Truman recognized the new nation on the same day.

WHAT IS A GENERATION?

"As for the days of our life, they contain seventy years, or if due to strength, eighty years, yet their pride is but labor and sorrow; for soon it is gone, and we fly away" (Ps. 90:10). This verse tells us that eighty years is the longest average of a generation of people; therefore, the possible date for Christ's return is 2028 (1948 + 80) per this literal parable. But is it literal? I will let you decide.

CHAPTER 18

EVENTS OF END-TIME PROPHECY TODAY

FOUR TYPES OF INTERPRETING PROPHECY AND TIMING

1. *Current tribulation believers* —They believe that tribulation began at Jesus's crucifixion and continues to this day. They believe these tribulations happen closer together and more intensely as we get closer to the Second Coming.
2. *Pretribulation believers*—They believe that a seven-year tribulation begins after the great mystery Paul tells us about in 1 Corinthians 15:51–55, known to most as the Rapture.
3. *Midtribulation believers*—They believe that the great mystery, the Rapture, happens in the middle of a seven-year tribulation period.
4. *Posttribulation Believers*—They believe that the great mystery, the Rapture, happens at the end of the seven-year tribulation.

All four types believe in the Second Coming of Christ. They all believe there will be a tribulation period. They all believe in the great mystery of transfiguration. The only difference in these beliefs is what they believe about the timing of Jesus's return.

As we discussed in the first lesson, God never does anything unless He reveals it first to his servants. He did just that through His Son during His time with the apostles. Matthew 24 and Luke 21 are the most referred to prophecies other than Revelation. What Jesus tells his apostles is parallel to the opening of the seals in Revelation 6. The wisest man in history, King Solomon, tells us in Ecclesiastes 3:15 that history repeats itself.

The disciples of Jesus came up to show Him the buildings of the temple, and Jesus said to them, "Do you not see all these things? Assuredly, I say to you, not one stone shall be left here upon another, that shall not be thrown down" (Matt. 24:1). Then the disciples asked Him, "When will these things be?" They also asked, "What will be the sign of Your coming, and the end of the age?" Then Jesus gives them a series of signs to look for: "And Jesus answered and said to them, 'See to it that no one misleads you. For many will come in My name, saying "I am the Christ," and will mislead many'" (Matt. 24:4–5).

> Then if anyone says to you, "Behold, he is the Christ,", or "There He is," do not believe him. For false Christs and false prophets will arise and will show great signs and wonders, so as to mislead, if possible, even the elect. Behold, I have told you in advance. So, if they say to you, "Behold, He is in the wilderness," do not go out, or "Behold, He is in the inner rooms," do not believe them." (Matt. 24:23–26)

Jesus tells us that one of the first signs of his return will be a false Christ and false prophets. This tells me that there will be a lot of counterfeits, as well as misinterpretations of scripture. The false Christ and false prophets will show great signs and wonders to deceive, if possible, God's chosen people.

Jesus said, "Then if any man shall say unto you, Lo, here is Christ, or there; believe it not." (Matt. 24:23). The way I interpret this is the false Christ does not necessarily have to admit to being Christ, but others will convince you.

Many books have been written about prophecy and end of days, but just because there is a best-selling book that talks about prophecy does not mean it is the truth. Always check facts with scripture. Not knowing your scripture could cause you to believe in a misinterpretation.

In my own lifetime, there have been false Christs and false prophets. For example, Jimmy Jones was an American preacher who conspired with his inner circle to direct a mass murder-suicide of his followers in the jungle commune at Jonestown, Guyana. A total of 909 people died in the wake of following this false preacher.

David Koresh claimed to be Christ. Koresh was the head of the Branch Davidians sect, which played a central role in the Waco siege of 1993. Seventy-nine Branch Davidians perished in the siege, twenty-one of them children. His believers said David Koresh had done great miracles and gave them great signs of the coming Armageddon, which caused them to believe him to be Christ.

Recently, there was a report from ABC News called *I Am the Son of God*. This report showed at least four people today with many followers, who claim to be the coming Messiah. This report is easy enough to find. Do a search on YouTube for "I am the Son of God by ABC news" and watch it. Most Christians would think this crazy. But there are really people out there who believe the Messiah is here or has been recently.

WARS AND RUMORS OF WAR

"You will be hearing of *wars and rumors of war*. See that you are not frightened, for those things must take place, but that is not the end. For nation will rise against nation, and kingdom against kingdom" (Matt. 24:6–7a; Luke 21:10; Rev. 6:3–4; emphasis mine).

Another sign Jesus gave for the last days was that there would be wars and rumors of wars. These wars and the other signs, Jesus told us, would be more frequent and intense. We know this because it is written that the day of the Lord will come suddenly "like a woman in labor" (1 Thess. 5:2–3). A woman's labor becomes more intense and closer together before the baby comes. "But all these things are merely the beginning of birth pangs" (Matt. 24:8).

Today, we do have wars and rumors of war. In addition, the world has an arsenal of nuclear weapons. There is clear and present danger in our world. There are countries in which people and soldiers are trained to be martyrs who are willing to use explosives that will blow them up as part of the horrific process of terrorizing others. Think of them having a nuclear weapon. With the stockpile of nuclear weapons today and the unrest in the world, our doomsday clock is closer than it was during the Cold War.

We also have chemical agents, nerve agents, and biological warfare. In the last century, there were several wars, including World War I; World War II; the Korean War; the Vietnam War; Desert Shield and Desert Storm; Enduring Freedom and Iraqi Freedom. These wars were only the wars in which the US was a participant. During this time period, other wars have been simultaneously taking place in the world at large. These wars have ravaged this planet, which God created for us to tend and keep (Gen. 2:15).

Furthermore, it is possible that if Jesus does not come soon, men will self-destruct. Do we not have the capacity to destroy ourselves? Jesus said in Matthew 24:22, "Unless those days were shortened, no flesh would survive." We are getting to that point.

NATURAL DISASTERS

Another sign Jesus gave us of the last days was an acceleration of natural disasters. There is a prophecy in Luke 21 where Jesus is talking about the signs of the end, just like in Matthew 24. He makes this additional statement: "And there will be signs in the sun and the moon and in the stars and on the earth, distress of nations with perplexity, the sea and the waves roaring." Have we seen that? And then you read on, "Men's hearts failing them for fear and the expectation of those things that are coming on the earth for the powers of heaven will be shaken" (Luke 21:26).

Just think about the past few years alone and the frequency of hurricanes, cyclones, tornadoes, winds, and floods. Do these events seem more intense and frequent? Here are some examples: December

26, 2004, one of the largest earthquakes ever recorded happened in an undersea fault in the Indian Ocean. This earthquake caused a series of tsunamis. The tsunamis were the deadliest in recorded history, taking 230,000 lives in a matter of hours.

In September 2017, a Category 5 hurricane, Maria, hit Puerto Rico. The official death toll was sixty-four, but the devastation and stories from local hospitals hint at a much larger amount. Researchers from Harvard's T. H. Chan School of Health discovered that in the months following Maria, the death rate was 62 percent higher than the year prior. This data made Maria the second deadliest hurricane in US history. It claimed more lives than Hurricane Katrina and 9/11 combined.

Jesus also talks about the acceleration of earthquakes. He says there will be earthquakes in diverse places. Since the United States Geological Survey (USGS) began monitoring earthquakes, they have been becoming more frequent and intense. All one needs to do is get on their website (earthquakes.usgs.gov) to see for themselves.

FAMINE AND PESTILENCE

The scriptures also say, "and in various places there will be famines" (Matt. 24:7b) and "and various places plagues and famines" (Luke 21:11), parallel to Revelation 6:7–8.

Another sign Jesus gave for the last days is famine. We still have people starving around the world today. According to the World Hunger Statistics, every day too many men and women across the globe struggle to feed their children a nutritious meal. In a world where we produce enough food to feed everyone, 821 million people, one in nine, still go to bed each night with an empty stomach! Even more, one in three suffer from some form of malnutrition. Jesus said there will be famines in different places, and this is the beginning of sorrows.

Pestilence can also be found in diverse places. Contagious diseases have shaped human history, and they remain with us today. As the 2019

Novel Coronavirus (COVID-19) spreads across mainland China and around the globe, such infectious diseases, have become the forefront of our thinking for many.

Here is a look at some of the worst of these infections:

1. ***2019 Novel Coronavirus***—In December 2019, COVID-19, a new strain of coronavirus first appeared in Wuhan, China. Though it was only recently discovered, 2019-nCoV, has already spread rapidly in China and around the world. At the time of this writing, there are 111 million confirmed cases and 2.45 million deaths related to COVID-19 in the world. In the US, 28 million have been infected, and there have been 494,000 deaths attributed to COVID-19.

2. ***Plague***—This ancient killer is still with us. Caused by a bacterium carried by fleas, plague has been blamed for decimating societies including fourteenth-century Europe during the Black Death, when it wiped out roughly a third of the population, including in Basel, Switzerland. The disease comes in three forms, but the best known is the bubonic plague, which is marked by buboes, or painfully swollen lymph nodes. Though antibiotics developed in the 1940s can treat the disease, in those who are left untreated, plague can have a fatality rate of 50 to 60 percent, the World Health Organization said. It has been reported that even today we have an average of seven cases each year in the US.

3. ***Malaria***—Although it is preventable and curable, malaria has devastated parts of Africa, where, according to the World Health Organization, the disease accounts for 20 percent of all childhood deaths. It is also present on other continents. Before progressing on to more serious complications, malaria is characterized by fever, chills, and flulike symptoms. The parasite that causes the disease is carried by blood-sucking mosquitoes. By 1951, with the help of the pesticide DDT, the disease was eliminated by the US.

4. *Influenza*—A seasonal respiratory infection, the flu, according to the World Health Organization, is responsible for about three million to five million cases of severe illness and about 250,000 to 500,000 deaths a year across the globe. Periodically, however, the viral infection becomes much more devastating. A pandemic in 1918 killed about fifty million people worldwide. As became apparent from the "swine flu" and "bird flu" scares in recent years, some influenza viruses can jump between species.

5. *HIV and AIDS*—At the end of 2018, about 37.9 million people were living with a human immunodeficiency virus (HIV) infection worldwide, 25.7 millions of those individuals are in Africa. About 770,000 people worldwide died from HIV and AIDS in 2018; 49,000 of those deaths were in the Americas, according to WHO.

6. *Cholera*—Cholera causes acute diarrhea that, if left untreated, can kill within hours. People catch the disease by eating or drinking substances containing the bacterium Vibrio cholerae. The bacteria tend to contaminate food and water through infected feces. Since symptoms can take twelve hours to five days to show, people can unwittingly spread the disease through their feces. Thanks to improved sanitation, cases of cholera have been rare in industrialized nations for the last hundred years. But according to WHO, worldwide it kills between 21,000 and 143,000 individuals every year. However, WHO says that during the nineteenth century, cholera spread from its home in India, causing six pandemics and killing millions of people on all continents. According to a report published in the Journal of Infectious Diseases, most recently, a cholera outbreak in Haiti, which began after that country's devastating 2010 earthquake, has to date sickened more than 810,000 people and killed nearly 9,000.

Some theologians believe the black horse in Revelation 6:5–6 is an economic disaster. This COVID-19 pandemic could be cause for concern. As the virus has traveled around the world, every country has been affected economically.

Prior to the pandemic, famine was at an all-time high. However, today, deaths from famine have increased. According to *Time* magazine, the disruption to food production and supplied because of COVID-19 could cause even more deaths from starvation than the disease itself.

The report stated that 121 million more people could be "pushed to the brink of starvation this year" as a result of the disruption in food production and supplies, as well as unemployment.

MARTYRS

"Then they will deliver you to tribulation, and will kill you, and you will be hated by all nations because of My name" (Mat. 24:9). See also Luke 21:12 and Revelation 6:9–11.

The first Christian martyr was disciple Stephen in Acts 7, and they have continued throughout history to this day. In some countries today, Christians are in a genocide situation. According to US Foreign Secretary Jeremy Hunt, "the persecution of Christians in parts of the world is near "genocide' levels."

VIOLENCE

"Because lawlessness is increased, most people's love will grow cold. But the one who endures to *the end*, he will be saved. This gospel of the kingdom shall be preached in the whole world as a testimony to all the nations, and then the end will come" (Matt. 24:12–14; emphasis mine).

In the days of Noah, it is written that the thoughts of men's hearts were continually evil and that violence filled the earth (Gen. 6:5). We have a great deal of violence today. Protests, vandalism, and even murder of the innocent.

We live in a time where abortion is allowed, even when a child has been born and is breathing. I believe this to be murder. Millions of unborn children have been murdered through abortion. Other atrocities destroying children's lives include child trafficking and child abuse.

I believe there is great tribulation today. Divorce, abuse, adultery, and other family crises are commonplace. Society is wrecked with the tribulations of famine, disease, and economic crisis. The tribulations become more and more frequent and intense before Christ's coming. Blessedly, the elect will be spared judgment at the last trumpet (1 Cor. 15:51–55).

SIGNS IN THE SUN, MOON AND STARS

"And there shall be signs in the sun, and in the moon, and in the stars" (Luke 21:25). We have seen such signs. Here are a few signs in the sun, moon, and stars within this decade alone:

- November 28, 2013—Comet ISON came closest to the sun on Hanukkah
- April 15, 2014—blood moon on Passover
- October 8, 2014—blood moon on the Feast of Trumpets
- March 20, 2015—solar eclipse during the Jewish New Year of the Kings
- April 4, 2015—blood moon, again on Passover
- September 13, 2015—solar eclipse, again on the Feast of Trumpets
- September 28, 2015—blood moon on the Feast of Tabernacle
- September 23, 2017—star constellation Virgo, Latin for virgin, appeared with twelve stars.

A note on the last bullet point: Normally Virgo has only nine stars; however, three planets—Mercury, Venus, and Mars—appears over her head. The king planet, Jupiter, had gestated for forty-two months and appears to come from Virgo. Some saw this as the sign given in Revelation 12:1–2.

Here are more examples, this time of the roaring of the sea and the waves (Luke 21:25).

With a damage total of at least $294.92 billion US dollars, the 2017 Atlantic hurricane season was both a hyperactive cyclone season and one of the costliest on record. This season featured seventeen named storms, ten hurricanes, and six major hurricanes. Tying with the year 1936, it was the fifth most active hurricane season on record.

Most of the season's damage was due to three hurricanes: Harvey, Irma, and Maria. Another notable hurricane, Nate, was the worst natural disaster in Costa Rican history. Following this season, because of the number of deaths and the amount of damage the storms caused, the names Harvey, Irma, Maria, and Nate were retired. Collectively, the tropical cyclones were responsible for at least 3,364 deaths. This was the most fatalities in a single season since 2005. Along with three record hurricanes—Irma, Harvey, and Maria—each generating an Accumulated cyclone energy (ACE) of over twenty, the season also had the highest accumulated cyclone energy since 2005.

The 2017 season was also one of only seven years on record to feature multiple Category 5 hurricanes and the only season other than 2007 with two hurricanes making landfall at that intensity. It also became the second consecutive season to feature at least one Category 5 hurricane, with Hurricane Matthew reaching such strength in the previous season. All ten of the season's hurricanes occurred in a row, the greatest number of consecutive hurricanes in the satellite era and tied for the highest number of consecutive hurricanes ever observed in the Atlantic Basin.

KNOWLEDGE WILL INCREASE

One of the most incredible signs that we will live in the end is a prophecy in Daniel 12. The angel says to Daniel, "But you Daniel, shut up the words and seal the book until the time of the end. Many will run to and fro and knowledge will increase." (Dan. 12:4)

People today are going to and fro faster than ever before. If you told someone a hundred years ago that it would soon be possible to travel across the world in one day, they would have locked you up. It was unthinkable.

The scripture says many will run to and fro and knowledge will increase. Are we living in that day? In this century, we have seen knowledge explode exponentially, more than it has in any other generation in human history.

SPREADING OF THE GOSPEL

Jesus made another prophecy that cannot be misunderstood. Speaking of the last days, He said, "And the gospel of this kingdom will be preached in all the world for a witness unto all nations and then the end will come" (Matt. 24:14). Did Jesus say He *might* come? No. Could come? May come? No. *Will* come! Is the Gospel being preached in all the world? He did not say they will all believe. He said, "For a witness, an opportunity." This is being fulfilled right now with internet access.

It is time to look up: "But when these things begin to take place straighten up and lift up your heads, because your redemption is drawing near" (Luke 21:28). "For then there will be a great tribulation, such as has not occurred since the beginning of the world until now, nor ever will. Unless those days had been cut short, no life would have been saved; but for the sake of the elect those days will be cut short" (Matthew 24:21, 22).

If we are truly living in the last days, are you ready for Jesus's glorious return?

> But immediately after the tribulation of those days the sun will be darkened, and the moon will not give its light, and the stars will fall from the sky, and the powers of the heavens will be shaken. And then the sign of the Son of Man will appear in the sky, and then all the tribes of the earth will mourn, and they will see the Son of Man coming on the clouds of the sky with power

and great glory. And He will send forth His angels with a great trumpet and they will gather together His elect from the four winds, from one end of the sky to the other. (Matt. 24:29–31; see also "The Wrath of the Lamb," Rev. 6:12–17).

There is only one trumpet left to blow. Are you ready?

Behold, I tell you a mystery, we will not all sleep, but we will all be changed, in a moment, in the twinkling of an eye, *at the last trumpet*; for the trumpet will sound, and the dead will be raised imperishable, and we will be changed. For this perishable must put on the imperishable and this mortal must put on immortality. (1 Cor. 15:51–53; Rev. 1:7; emphasis mine)

For this we say to you by the Word of the Lord, that we who are alive and remain until the coming of the Lord, will not precede those who have fallen asleep. For the Lord Himself will descend from heaven with a shout, with the voice of the archangel and *with the trumpet of God*, and the dead in Christ will rise first. Then we who are alive and remain we will be caught up together with them in the clouds to meet the Lord in the air, and so we shall always be with the Lord. (1 Thess. 4:16–17; emphasis mine)

When will the last trumpet sound?

This is the will of Him who sent Me that of all that He has given Me I lose nothing but raise it up on *the last day*. For this is the will of my Father, that everyone who beholds the Son and believes in Him will have eternal life, and I, Myself will raise him up on *the last day*. (John 6:39–40; emphasis mine)

John 6 goes on to say, "No one can come to Me unless the Father who sent Me draws him; and I will raise him up on *the last day*" (John 6:44) and "He who eats My flesh and drinks My blood has eternal life, and I will raise him up on *the last day*" (John 6:54).

CHAPTER 19

CREATION AND TIME

SYMBOLIC MESSAGE

With God, a day is like a thousand years and a thousand years is like a day: "But, beloved, be not ignorant of this one thing, that one day is with the Lord as a thousand years, and a thousand years as one day" (2 Pet. 3:8).

When I first began reading Genesis, with the limited knowledge of scripture that I had, it really messed with my brain. I took scripture completely literally. I had no problem with God creating the heavens and earth in six days and resting on the seventh. However, when it came to Adam and Eve and their children, things just did not add up. How could Cain, one of the sons of Adam and Eve, who rose up and slew his brother Abel, be banished to the land of Nod, marry a woman, have a child named Enoch, and name a city after his son *if* Adam, Eve, Abel, and Cain were the first four people on the planet?

After some in-depth study, I found my answer. It is my hope that this explanation helps others who might have the same question.

Moses was on Mount Sinai for forty days with God, who gave Moses His laws and the Ten Commandments. First, God wanted Moses to know just who the great I AM was, the *Creator*. Then God begins *His timeline*. It is this timeline that has great importance when studying prophecy. Let us begin our study of Genesis chapters 1 and 2, with time and prophecy.

Daily Symbolic Meaning

If a day is a thousand years to God, each day would be considered a thousand years.

Day One

> And God said, let there be light: and there was light. And God saw the light, that it was good: and God divided the light from the darkness. And God called the light Day, and the darkness he called Night. And the evening and the morning were the first day. (Gen. 1:1–5)

On day one, God creates light, calling the light day and the dark night, dividing the two. What is this light? It cannot be the sun, as it was not created until day four.

"Then spake *Jesus* again unto them, saying, *I am the light of the world*: he that followeth me shall not walk in darkness, but shall have the light of life" (John 8:12; emphasis mine). This verse hints that Jesus is the light. However, the light cannot be Jesus Himself. Why? Because "[a]ll things were made by Him; and without Him was not anything made that was made" (John 1:3). This means Jesus was with God during creation, so He could not be created.

Let us look at what else this light could it be: "In the beginning was the word, and the word was with God, and the word was God" (John 1:1). "And the Word was made flesh, and dwelt among us, (and we beheld his glory, the glory as of the only begotten of the Father,) full of grace and truth" (John 1:14).

In the beginning was the Word, which was the light, and it was this Word which became flesh (Jesus) and dwelled among us. Therefore, symbolically, the first thing God creates is His Word. The Word, Jesus, and God are one. One thousand years is up.

Adam received the first word when God breathed the "breath of life" into his nostrils.

Day Two

> And God said, Let there be a firmament in the midst of
> the waters, and let it divide the waters from the waters.
> And God made the firmament and divided the waters
> which were under the firmament from the waters which
> were above the firmament: and it was so. And God
> called the firmament Heaven. And the evening and the
> morning were the second day. (Gen. 1:6–8)

This is the only day of creation in which God did *not* say, "It was good."
If we go back to our symbolic meanings, we know waters to represent
people, nations, and tongues. "And he saith unto me, The waters which
thou sawest, where the whore sitteth, are peoples, and multitudes, and
nations, and tongues" (Rev. 17:15).

Here God is dividing the waters and putting a firmament between
them. The firmament is called heaven. In this symbolic message, God
is dividing the people, those in heaven and those not. There are two
types of people, those who are with God and those who oppose Him.
Two thousand years are up.

It was during the time of Noah that the waters (people) were
divided. Noah, Noah's wife, his sons and his sons wives, divided from
a sinful world.

Day Three

> And God said, Let the waters under the heaven be
> gathered together unto one place, and let the dry land
> appear: and it was so. And God called the dry land
> Earth; and the gathering together of the waters called
> the Seas: and God saw that *it was good*. And God said,
> Let the earth bring forth grass, the herb yielding seed,
> and the fruit tree yielding fruit after his kind, whose
> seed is in itself, upon the earth: and it was so. And the
> earth brought forth grass, and herb yielding seed after

his kind, and the tree yielding fruit, whose seed was in itself, after his kind: and God saw that it was good. And the evening and the morning were the third day. (Gen. 1:9–13; emphasis mine)

Here God is separating the waters from the earth, with the earth having seeds that produce yielding fruit. From our symbols we know a tree to represent a cross or people and nation: "The righteous shall flourish like the palm tree: he shall grow like a cedar in Lebanon" (Ps. 92:12); "I have seen the wicked in great power and spreading himself like a green bay tree" (Ps. 37:35).

A seed is either a descendant or Jesus, and as we saw in day one, Jesus and the Word are one (John 1:1). It is Jesus Himself who tells us about the sewing of the seed (God's Word):

Hear ye therefore the parable of the sower. When any one heareth the word of the kingdom, and understandeth it not, then cometh the wicked one, and catcheth away that which was sown in his heart. This is he which received seed by the wayside. But he that received the seed into stony places, the same is he that heareth the word, and anon with joy receiveth it; Yet hath he not root in himself, but dureth for a while: for when tribulation or persecution ariseth because of the word, by and by he is offended. He also that received seed among the thorns is he that heareth the word; and the care of this world, and the deceitfulness of riches, choke the word, and he becometh unfruitful. But he that received seed into the good ground is he that heareth the word, and understandeth it; which also beareth fruit, and bringeth forth, some an hundredfold, some sixty, some thirty. (Matt. 13:18–23)

Here in day three, the symbolic meaning is that God is separating those who have the Word and are productive from the rest of the world. Three thousand years gone.

Abraham, the father of many nations, carried the seed through the generations, to Jesus.

Day Four

> And God said, Let there be lights in the firmament of the heaven to divide the day from the night; and let them be for signs, and for seasons, and for days, and years: And let them be for lights in the firmament of the heaven to give light upon the earth: and it was so. And God made two great lights; the greater light to rule the day, and the lesser light to rule the night: he made the stars also. And God set them in the firmament of the heaven to give light upon the earth, And to rule over the day and over the night, and to divide the light from the darkness: and God saw that it was good. And the evening and the morning were the fourth day. (Gen. 1:14–19)

The great light that rules the day is God, Jesus, and the Word, and the lesser light that rules the darkness is, sin and Satan. We are the children of the light, not of the darkness. "Ye are all the children of light, and the children of the day: we are not of the night, nor of darkness" (1 Thess. 5:5).

The lights in the firmament are stars, which are God's messengers, angels of the church: "The seven stars are the angels of the seven churches" (Rev. 1:20b).

On day four, our symbolic message is that we are either children of the day, God's people, or children of the night, Satan's. We have that choice. The stars are those who share God's message of salvation. Furthermore, we only have a set time, as the sun, moon, and stars are there to tell time, "seasons, days and years." Jesus came the first time "in the fulness of time" and will again. Four thousand years are up.

Moses was given the word by God, seen as the sun, to the Israelites, seen as the moon that reflex the sun. The Levite priests were the stars, who were to spread the message.

Day Five

> And God said, Let the waters bring forth abundantly the moving creature that hath life, and fowl that may fly above the earth in the open firmament of heaven. And God created great whales, and every living creature that moveth, which the waters brought forth abundantly, after their kind, and every winged fowl after his kind: and God saw that it was good. And God blessed them, saying, Be fruitful, and multiply, and fill the waters in the seas, and let fowl multiply in the earth. And the evening and the morning were the fifth day. (Gen. 1:20–23)

Wings refer to speed, protection, or deliverance: "The LORD shall bring a nation against thee from far, from the end of the earth, as swift as the eagle flieth; a nation whose tongue thou shalt not understand (Deut. 28:49); "O Jerusalem, Jerusalem, thou that killest the prophets, and stonest them which are sent unto thee, how often would I have gathered thy children together, even as a hen gathereth her chickens under her wings, and ye would not" (Matt. 23:37).

The beast, which is kingdom or governmental power under the control of Satan, lives in the sea: "And I stood upon the sand of the sea, and saw a beast rise up out of the sea, having seven heads and ten horns, and upon his horns ten crowns, and upon his heads the name of blasphemy" (Rev. 13:1).

On day five, our symbolic message is simple: we are either under the protection of the wings of God or living in the sea (worldly) with Satan lives. Five thousand years are up.

King David protected his people, as an eagle protects his children, under his wing.

Day Six

> And God said, Let the earth bring forth the living creature after his kind, cattle, and creeping thing, and beast of the earth after his kind: and it was so. And God made the beast of the earth after his kind, and cattle after their kind, and everything that creepeth upon the earth after his kind: and God saw that it was good. And God said, Let us make man in our image, after our likeness: and let them have dominion over the fish of the sea, and over the fowl of the air, and over the cattle, and over all the earth, and over every creeping thing that creepeth upon the earth. So, God created man in his own image, in the image of God created he him; male and female created he them. And God blessed them, and God said unto them, Be fruitful, and multiply, and replenish the earth, and subdue it: and have dominion over the fish of the sea, and over the fowl of the air, and over every living thing that moveth upon the earth. And God said, Behold, I have given you every herb bearing seed, which is upon the face of all the earth, and every tree, in the which is the fruit of a tree yielding seed; to you it shall be for meat. And to every beast of the earth, and to every fowl of the air, and to everything that creepeth upon the earth, wherein there is life, I have given every green herb for meat: and it was so. And God saw everything that he had made, and, behold, it was very good. And the evening and the morning were the sixth day. (Gen. 1:24–31)

Here on day six, the symbolic message is still explaining the division of the two types of people, those in the image of God, doing God's will, and those living with the beast and doing his will. See Is. 53:6. Six thousand years are up.

Jesus, God in the flesh, came as a man, to save the world from sin.

Seventh Day

> Thus the heavens and the earth were finished, and all the host of them. And on the seventh day God ended his work which he had made; and he rested on the seventh day from all his work which he had made. And God blessed the seventh day and sanctified it: because that in it he had rested from all his work which God created and made. (Gen. 2:1–3)

On this glorious seventh day, God rests from all His creation, blessing the day and sanctifying it. Seven thousand years gone. What is this message? The seventh day is when God will set up His kingdom for one thousand years and then rest.

The seventh day is symbolic of the millennium reign of Jesus.

Symbolic Timeline in Genesis 1:

Adam/Word	Noah/Divided Water	Abram/Seed of Jesus	Moses/Priests	David/Wing of Protection	Jesus/God in the flesh	Millenium Rest
Day One	Day Two	Day Three	Day Four	Day Five	Day Six	Day Seven

CHAPTER 20

CREATION AND TIME

LITERAL MESSAGE

I am not Einstein—not even close. I do, however, have my own simple short theory.

Day One

On the first day, God creates light. In my opinion, the first thing God would want to do (scientifically) is to ensure that life can be sustained. The only literal light that I know we can see is the sun, moon, and stars. As we have discussed, these were not created until day four. However, there is a light that we cannot see that helps sustain life on Earth. It is in our core. It is this core that creates our known atmosphere and gives us sustainable air.

Day Two

How I see it, on day two God creates a life-sustaining planet. The thousand years are past, and the Earth is slowly moving closer to the sun. We know the core is full of magma, and as it gets closer to the sun, it begins heating up and spinning. This frozen rock called Earth begins to form, and the steam from the heat of the core expands, separating the waters. There is mist below and steam above. Two thousand years later, God has made the Earth spin.

Day Three

After two thousand years, as God puts a spin on things, He nudges Earth even closer to the sun. The spin pulls the waters below away from the Earth, allowing God to create his seed-bearing plants and trees on the solid earth. It was between the three thousandth year and the four thousandth year when the Earth was seeded and planted.

Day Four

On day four, God places His newly created life-sustaining planet right where He wants it. It is the third rock from the sun. God places the Earth here for the purpose of signs, seasons, days, and years. His plan (in my opinion) was to place Earth in just enough sunlight to help with the growth of His creation. This has now taken four thousand years.

Day Five

God then creates living creatures in the sea and the fowl of the air. Birds help with the spreading of the seeds of God's created seed-bearing trees and plants. The fish will soon be a food source for future creations. The creation of living sea animals and fowl took us to five thousand years.

Day Six

God created the creeping things to help pollenate the seed-bearing trees and plants, cattle as a future food source, and beasts to keep things in balance. Then God, with all His mercy and grace, created us, *mankind*, in His image. "Male and Female He made them" (Gen. 1:27). Six thousand years. Mankind can now live on a breathable planet, eating off the seed-bearing plants, and consuming the fish of the sea and the cattle. Life is great! Right? On the six thousandth year, God created mankind in His image. God gives this planet and everything in it to mankind.

And God blessed them, and God said unto them, Be fruitful, and multiply, and replenish the earth, and subdue it: and have dominion over the fish of the sea, and over the fowl of the air, and over every living thing that moveth upon the earth. And God said, Behold, I have given you every herb bearing seed, which is upon the face of all the earth, and every tree, in the which is the fruit of a tree yielding seed; to you it shall be for meat. And to every beast of the earth, and to every fowl of the air, and to everything that creepeth upon the earth, wherein there is life, I have given every green herb for meat: and it was so. (Gen. 1:28–30)

Day Seven

Looking back on His creation and blessing the seventh thousandth year, behold, on the "seventh day," God rests.

CHAPTER 21

ADAM AND THE BREATH OF LIFE

GENESIS 2

I reference herewith my questioning of Cain being banished to Nod, marrying, and having a child, Enoch. Cain builds a city, naming it after his first son, Enoch. Simply, there had been plenty of time for mankind to be fruitful and multiply in the thousand years after they were created and in the thousand years of God's rest.

After creation in Genesis 1, we can see a shift in the creation story as Genesis 2 begins. We are not given a timeframe between the seventh day of rest and the time of the new message God is giving Moses in chapter 2.

Here God forms a man from the dust of the ground. In Hebrew, the word *dust* is '*âphâr*, which means "clay." As we have seen in our past studies, God forms His people like a potter forms his clay.

> The word which came to Jeremiah from the Lord, saying: "Arise and go down to the potter's house, and there I will cause you to hear My words." Then I went down to the potter's house, and there he was making something at the wheel. And the vessel that he made of clay was marred in the hand of the potter; so, he made it again into another vessel, as it seemed good to the potter

to make. Then the word of the Lord came to me, saying: "O house of Israel, can I not do with you as the potter?" says the Lord. "Look, as the clay in the potter's hand, so are you in My hand, O house of Israel." (Jer. 18:1–6)

This means Adam was *formed* from created mankind in Genesis 1:27. What does God do next to this formed man? He breaths into his nostrils the breath of life, and this man becomes a "living soul." And what is this breath of life? "It is the spirit that quickeneth; the flesh profiteth nothing: the words that I speak unto you, they are spirit, and they are life" (John 6:63).

The word Jesus spoke is *life*. As we have seen in John 1:1 and John 1:14, Jesus, the Word, and God are all one: "In the beginning was the word, and the word was with God, and the word was God" (John 1:1). "And the word was made flesh, and dwelt among us, (and we beheld His glory as of the only begotten of the Father), full of grace and truth" (John 1:14).

There are three types of living and three types of death:

- First living is when you are born into this world and take your first breath, and the first dying is when you take your last breath.
- Second living is a spiritual life and death. When you accept God's Word and His Son, Jesus Christ, you are spiritually alive. The second spiritual death is the denial of these.
- Third living is our eternal life, either with our Father in heaven or in eternal damnation, the third death.

God chose to form this unique man and give him the Word of God. Then God planted a garden in the east of Eden and placed the man, who now had His Word, into this garden to tend it: "And the LORD God took the man and put him into the garden of Eden to dress it and to keep it" (Gen. 2:15).

In Genesis 2:5, we can see that plant and herbs in the field had yet to grow. This was because there was no one to till it: "for the LORD

God had not caused it to rain upon the earth, and there was not a man to till the ground" (Gen. 2:5).

What does the Word of God tell us about tilling the ground? In the book of Matthew, Jesus tells us exactly what it means with His parable of the sower (tiller):

> Hear ye therefore the parable of the sower. When any one heareth the word of the kingdom, and understandeth it not, then cometh the wicked one, and catcheth away that which was sown in his heart. This is he which received seed by the wayside. But he that received the seed into stony places, the same is he that heareth the word, and anon with joy receiveth it; Yet hath he not root in himself, but dureth for a while: for when tribulation or persecution ariseth because of the word, by and by he is offended. He also that received seed among the thorns is he that heareth the word; and the care of this world, and the deceitfulness of riches, choke the word, and he becometh unfruitful. But he that received seed into the good ground is he that heareth the word, and understandeth it; which also beareth fruit, and bringeth forth, some an hundredfold, some sixty, some thirty. (Matt. 13:18–23)

Because man had been fruitful and multiplied, as God had directed in Genesis 1:28, God gave His Word for Adam to spread. Now God wants mankind to know Him (their Creator).

How can we be certain it was the Word God gave Adam? First, we see the Word in the story of Cain and Abel, Adam and Eve's first two sons. They knew that an offering was expected. It was this offering that caused their conflict, as Abel gave a more acceptable offering to God, which caused Cain to become jealous, and he rose and slew his brother, Abel.

Furthermore, Noah had to know the difference between what was clean and what was unclean, as he took seven each of the clean beasts into the ark and two each of the unclean as God directed: "Of every clean beast thou shalt take to thee by sevens, the male and his female: and of beasts that are not clean by two, the male and his female" (Gen. 7:2).

After the flood when Noah found dry land, what was the first thing he did? He built an altar to the Lord and gave an offering:

> And Noah builded an altar unto the LORD; and took of every clean beast, and of every clean fowl, and offered burnt offerings on the altar. And the LORD smelled a sweet savour; and the LORD said in his heart, I will not again curse the ground any more for man's sake; for the imagination of man's heart is evil from his youth; neither will I again smite any more everything living, as I have done. (Gen. 8:20–21)

How would Noah know this was expected without the Word? From Genesis 5, we know Adam lived 930 years, dying only fifty-six years before Noah. He lived among his family, and surely he was spreading the Word of God, since he had paid the ultimate price for his disobedience to God (death). Per Genesis 3, Adam's disobedience to God when he ate the forbidden fruit caused death to all mankind, known as "the fall of man."

After forming Adam, God forms every beast in the field and the fowl of the air, bringing them to Adam to name. God formed the different species in what some call evolution.

Our starting point in prophecy and time, as we will see in our review, is Adam's story in Genesis 2 and 3.

CHAPTER 22

REVIEW

I am convinced that creation was not six days, but six thousand years, as a day is like a thousand years, and a thousand years is a day to God. On the seventh thousandth year, God rests.

Birth of Adam		Birth of Noah		Birth of Abraham		Birth of Isaac		Birth of Jacob	Entered Egypt Jacob 130 yrs. old	Years In Egypt	Exodus	Solomon 4th Yr. Reign
4114BC	1056 Yrs.	3058BC	892 Yrs.	2166BC	100 Yrs.	2066BC	60 Yrs.	2006BC	1876BC	430 Yrs.	1446BC	966BC

Solomon's Reign

4114 BC–966 BC

From our previous studies, we see that Adam was born in 4114 BC, per scripture and simple addition. The above table gives us the timeframe between Adam and the reign of Solomon.

966 BC–539 BC

After King Solomon, the monarchy was divided into two kingdoms, the northern kingdom of Israel and the southern kingdom of Judah. Because of the disobedience of God's people, in the year 722 BC, the northern kingdom of Israel was destroyed by the Assyrians. Then in 538 BC, the southern kingdom of Judah was carried away to Babylon.

Daniels image interpretation in chapter 2, expanded in chapter 7

605 BC–539 BC

Babylon is the head of gold that reigned between 605 BC–539 BC.

539 B.C–331 B.C

Medo-Persia, the chest and arms of silver, conquered Cyrus the Great of Babylon in 539 BC.

331 BC–168 BC

Greece, the belly and thighs of bronze, was conquered by Alexander the Great, who is considered one of the greatest military minds of all time. Their weapons were made of bronze.

168 BC– AD 476

On June 22 in 168 BC, during the Battle of Pydna, Rome (the legs of iron) became the new great kingdom of iron, reigning from 168 BC to AD 476. This kingdom was ruling when Jesus was nailed to the cross.

AD 409–AD 910

Eventually the empire was divided into ten barbarian kingdoms. Historically, the period of the barbarian kingdoms spans between AD 409 and AD 910. Symbolically they are part iron and part clay, ten toes. The ten barbarian kingdoms are as follows:

- Alemanni—German
- Burgundians—Swiss
- Franks – French

- Lombards—Italian
- Saxons—English
- Suebi— Portuguese
- Visigoths—Spanish
- Heruli—Extinct
- Ostrogoths—Extinct
- Vandals—Extinct

AD 538–AD 1798

The 1,260 years—time, times, and dividing of time is forty-two months or 1260 days.

The Roman church-state power became supreme in Christendom in AD 538. This corrupted church and state began its rule in AD 538, but in 1798, Napoleon Bonaparte did not want to take orders from this united church and state and sent his top general, General Berthier, to arrest the pope and claim Rome. He took their power away.

Ad 1776–Present

These are the days of the beast with two horns that spoke like a lamb. On July 4, 1776, the United States of America gained independence, and by 1790, all thirteen colonies had ratified the Constitution. This nation was quickly drawn into world politics and today is a world superpower. This great power has slowly become the new Babylon.

1947–1948

Israel became a nation once again, as seen in the parable of the fig tree.

1949–1950

There were four consecutive red moons on Israel's holy feast days. The Arab-Israeli War, when five Arab armies (Egypt, Syria, Jordan, Lebanon, and Iraq) invaded Israel, also took place.

1967

The year of the Six-Day War. Jerusalem is now Israel's. Four consecutive red moons on Israel's holy feast days. During the Six-Day War of June 5–10, 1967, the armies of Egypt, Jordan, Syria, and Lebanon (and later Iraq) attacked Israel. Their goal was to wipe Israel off the map, but instead the Jews gained full access to all of Jerusalem for the first time in nearly two thousand years!

2013

Comet ISON hurls around the sun. Some astronomers were convinced that it was on a direct path toward Earth, but it broke up in the sun's atmosphere.

2014–2015

Four consecutive red moons on Israel's holy feast days.

2016

Donald Trump became president of the little horn, great superpower, Babylon, against all odds.

December 6, 2017

Donald Trump recognizes Jerusalem as Israel's capital on Hanukkah.

2017–2019

The worst flooding, hurricanes, and natural disasters in history. News anchors claim them to be "biblical."

The plague of COIVD-19 spreads around the globe, causing economic problems, famine, and hysteria in the world. Riots, vandalism, murders are all increasing in frequencies and intensity.

From the time of Adam's birth, it has been 6,134 years. We are on the seventh day (seven thousandth), and it is the dawn of God's rest (His millennial reign).

It is time for God's people to stand up for their Creator, to recognize who He is and all that He has done for His chosen people. Grab your sword (the Word of God), as we are in a battle against the forces of evil in this world. Stand against Satan, the father of lies, proving his lies by God's Word.

No battle is won with only a defense, our shield of faith. God gives us a full armor to use in this battle. A helmet of salvation, a breastplate of righteousness, a waistband of truth, shoes of peace, and a sword for combat. Just like Jesus, when Satan comes—and he will—tell him to get behind you, because you have the Word of God, which kills the lies he throws at you. We are sealed with this Word between our eyes. With this seal we do God's will; without it, we fall into temptation.

> Put on the whole armour of God, that ye may be able to stand against the wiles of the devil. For we wrestle not against flesh and blood, but against principalities, against powers, against the rulers of the darkness of this world, against spiritual wickedness in high places. Wherefore take unto you the whole armour of God, that ye may be able to withstand in the evil day, and having done all, to stand. Stand therefore, having your loins girt about with truth, and having on the breastplate of righteousness; And your feet shod with the preparation of the gospel of peace; Above all, taking the shield of faith, wherewith ye shall be able to quench all the fiery darts of the wicked. And take the helmet of salvation, and the sword of the Spirit, which is the word of God. (Eph. 6:11–17)

CHAPTER 23

MY AWAKENING DREAM

In my prefix, I explained that my studies of prophecy began because of a dream that has directed this path.

In my dream, I had an awareness of my sleep state. It was as if I were watching myself sleep. In this dream, I was awakened by a voice. The voice spoke and said, "Come and see." Within my dream, I then got out of my bed and followed this voice to a picture window in the back of the house we presently live in and where I was sleeping. The dream continued.

I watched the eastern sky as a bright star began to blink. It moved closer and closer, growing brighter and brighter. Soon the light was pure white, glowing with multiple colors as if a rainbow surrounded the light. From the light, I heard a voice say, "I'm coming soon."

At this point in my dream, I began running down the hall of the house I grew up in as a teenager. It was still night as I ran through my parents' bedroom door to my mother's side of the bed. I called out to my mother, "Jesus is coming! Jesus is coming!" She immediately woke up, got down on her knees, and began to pray. Then I then ran to my dad's side of the bed. I began shaking him and screaming, "Jesus is coming! Jesus is coming!" He would not wake up. No matter how much I tried, I could not wake him. Tears began to run down my cheeks, and panic crept in as I woke up.

With real tears running down my cheeks and my heart racing, I tried to focus on the dream I'd just had. My understanding of the dream at that time was that I was to witness to my parents about the soon expected return of my Lord and Savior, Jesus Christ, which I did.

Eventually God revealed much more. He expected me to tell all the people I could that Jesus is coming, and soon. He revealed to me that some people will accept my witness and prepare themselves, but others will slumber, ignore my message, and be unprepared. In addition, by taking me back in time, He was wanting me to look in our past to see the future.

Who will you be? I pray that you will be ready, as the time is at hand and Jesus is coming!

The good news is this: All have sinned and done things that are displeasing to God (Rom. 3:23). There is no one who is innocent (Rom. 3:10–18). The consequence of sin is death (Rom. 6:23). But God demonstrated His love toward us while we were still sinners by sending His Son, Jesus Christ, to die for us (Rom. 5:8). The death of Jesus is payment in full for our sins. Confess with your mouth that Jesus is Lord and believe in your heart that God raised Him from the dead, and you will be saved (Rom. 10:9). Everyone who calls upon the name of Jesus will be saved (Rom. 10:13).

ADDITIONAL PROPHECY FULFILLMENTS BY JESUS

PROPHECIES FULFILLED BY JESUS

Below are many more prophecies fulfilled by our Lord, Jesus Christ— prophecies written years before His coming, found at the archaeological site of Qumran in the Judaean Desert, near the Dead Sea. They are known as the Dead Sea Scrolls.

The Messiah Will Be Born in Bethlehem

- Micah 5:2

The Fulfillment

- Matthew 2:1–6

The Messiah Will Be Born of a Virgin

- Isaiah 7:14

The Fulfillment

- Matthew 1:20–23

The Messiah Will Be a Prophet Like Moses

- Deuteronomy 18:15

The Fulfillment

- John 7:40–42
- Acts 3:20–23

The Messiah Will Be Tempted by Satan

- Psalm 91:10–12

The Fulfillment

- Matthew 4:5–7

THE MESSIAH WILL ENTER JERUSALEM TRIUMPHANTLY

- Zechariah 9:9

The Fulfillment

- Matthew 21:8–11
- Luke 19:35–37
- John 12:12–15

THE MESSIAH WILL BE REJECTED BY HIS OWN PEOPLE

- Isaiah 53:1, 3

The Fulfillment

- John 1:10–11
- John 12:37–38

THE MESSIAH WILL BE BETRAYED BY ONE OF HIS FOLLOWERS

- Psalm 41:9
- Psalm 55:12–13

The Fulfillment

- Matthew 26:47, 49–50a
- Luke 22:21–22, 47b
- John 13:18, 21, 26

The Messiah Will Be Betrayed for Thirty Pieces of Silver

- Zechariah 11:12–13

The Fulfillment

- Matthew 26:14–16
- Matthew 27:3–4a

The Messiah Will Be Tried and Condemned

- Isaiah 53:8

The Fulfillment

- Matthew 27:1–2
- Luke 23:1, 23
- Acts 4:26–28

The Messiah Will Be Silent Before His Accusers

- Psalm 35:11
- Isaiah 53:7–8a

The Fulfillment

- Matthew 27:12–14
- Mark 15:3–5
- 1 Peter 2:22–23

The Messiah Will Be Smitten and Spat Upon

- Micah 5:1
- Isaiah 50:6

The Fulfillment

- Matthew 26:67–68
- Matthew 27:30
- Mark 14:65a
- John 19:1–3

The Messiah Will Be Mocked and Taunted

- Psalm 22:7–8

The Fulfillment

- Matthew 27:39–40
- Luke 23:11, 35

The Messiah to Die By Crucifixion, With Pierced Hands And Feet

- Psalm 22:14-16
- Zechariah 12:10a

The Fulfillment

- Matthew 27:31
- Mark 15:20
- John 19:15–16

THE MESSIAH WILL SUFFER WITH SINNERS

- Isaiah 53:12a

The Fulfillment

- Matthew 27:38
- Mark 15:27
- Luke 23:32–33

THE MESSIAH'S GARMENTS WILL BE DIVIDED BY CASTING LOTS

- Psalm 22:18

The Fulfillment

- Matthew 27:35
- Mark 15:24
- John 19:23–24a

THE MESSIAH'S BONES WILL NOT BE BROKEN

- Numbers 9:12

The Fulfillment

- John 19:31–37

The Messiah Will Die as a Sin Offering

- Isaiah 53:5–6, 8, 12

The Fulfillment

- John 1:29
- Acts 10:43
- Acts 13:38–39
- 1 Corinthians 15:3–4
- Ephesians 1:7
- 1 Peter 2:24
- Revelation 1:5b

The Messiah Will See His Seed

- Isaiah 53:10–11

The Fulfillment

- Ephesians 1:4–5, 21–23
- Hebrews 12:2

The Messiah Will Be Buried in a Rich Man's Tomb

- Isaiah 53:9

The Fulfillment

- Matthew 27:57–60

THE MESSIAH WILL BE RAISED FROM THE DEAD

- Psalm 16:10
- Psalm 30:3

The Fulfillment

- Matthew 28:5–7
- Mark 16:6–7
- Acts 2:27–31
- 1 Corinthians 15:17, 20

THE MESSIAH WILL SIT AT GOD'S RIGHT HAND

- Psalm 110:1

The Fulfillment

- Mark 16:19
- Acts 2:32–36
- Hebrews 10:12–13

Printed in the United States
by Baker & Taylor Publisher Services